On
Stories

RICHARD KEARNEY

On
Stories

London and New York

First published 2002
by Routledge
2 Park Square, Milton Park, Abingdon, Oxon, OX14 4RN

Simultaneously published in the USA and Canada by Routledge
270 Madison Ave, New York NY 10016

Routledge is an imprint of the Taylor & Francis Group

Transferred to Digital Printing 2005

© 2002 Richard Kearney

Typeset in Joanna by RefineCatch Limited, Bungay, Suffolk

British Library Cataloguing in Publication Data
A catalogue record for this book is available from the British Library

Library of Congress Cataloging in Publication Data
Kearney, Richard
   On stories / Richard Kearney.
      p.   cm. – (Thinking in action)
   Includes bibliographical references and index.
      1. Prose literature – History and criticism.   2. Narration (Rhetoric)   I. Title.
   II. Series.
      PN3353 .K43   2001
      809 – dc21   2001031753

ISBN 0-415-24797-7 (hbk)
ISBN 0-415-24798-5 (pbk)

Printed and bound by Antony Rowe Ltd, Eastbourne

105,00

For
Anne Bernard

It was a stormy night in the Bay of Biscay and his sailors were seated around the fire. Suddenly the Captain said, Tell us a story, Captain. And the Captain began, It was a stormy night in the Bay of Biscay . . .

Ciaran Carson, **Fishing for Amber: A Long Story**

Preface

I gratefully remember here those who first introduced me to the life of stories. My grandfather, George, who told me the story of the Twelve Little Kids every time he came to visit our childhood home. My grandmother, Delia, for endlessly recounting her magical stories of Ballinrobe romance in her attic bedroom in our Cork house, where she came to recover after my grandfather's death and which she never left until her own death some twelve years later. I remember too my father, Kevin, who let my grandmother come to stay with us on the understanding that her heart condition gave her only months to live, but who was no mean storyteller in his own right, despite his demanding schedule as a busy surgeon. The tale of his I recall the best is that of a mysterious Jacky Dory, which lasted some ten seconds and went like this – 'I'll tell you a story about Jacky Dory . . . (pause) . . . and that is the end of the story.' My six siblings and I were fascinated by this story of the excluded middle and spent much of our time as children trying to draw the secret from our father – without success. I am also grateful to my mother, Ann, for reading to the family every night before we slept (weeping each time she read her favourite tale, 'The Happy Prince'). And passing on to a new generation, I would like to thank my two beautiful and resolute daughters, Simone and Sarah, who refused to sleep as children until I told them the story of the Twelve Little Kids, or a Ballinrobe romance, or 'Jacky Dory', or 'The Happy Prince', or other stories that never seemed to tire of being told.

My appreciation also goes to my editors Tony Bruce, Muna Khogali and Simon Critchley for their guidance and encouragement, and to those friends and colleagues who read the typescript and offered helpful comments and corrections – Kevin Whelan, Paul Freaney, Susan Brown, David Wood, William Desmond, David Rasmussen, John Cleary and Charles Guignon. Finally, a word of hearty appreciation to my inspiring graduate students at Boston College and University College Dublin for their enthusiasm and support, in particular, John Manoussakis, Matt Pelletier, Brian Peltonen and Bob Erlewine.

I would like also to beg in advance my readers' indulgence regarding my use of extensive notes. The decision to defer much of the more specialised philosophical discussion of narrative to endnotes is prompted by a desire to make the main text as accessible as possible to a non-specialist readership, in keeping with the spirit of this series. Only those wishing to consult the more academic sources behind the general argument need, therefore, concern themselves with the scholarly apparatus and addenda. I would, finally, like to express a regret that my political reading of the cinematic stories of 'strangers' in Part 3 did not allow scope for an appreciation of the more artistic qualities of these films. I hope that my emphasis on the poetic powers of storytelling in other sections of the book will make up for this. For it is my conviction that if narrative calls at times for critical and theoretical interpretation, it also enchants us with the sheer magic of imagination.

Part One
Where do Stories Come From?

Where do Stories Come From?

One

If this be magic, let it be an art lawful as eating.

A Winter's Tale

Telling stories is as basic to human beings as eating. More so, in fact, for while food makes us live, stories are what make our lives worth living. They are what make our condition human.

This was recognised from the very beginnings of Western civilisation. Hesiod tells us how the founding myths (mythos in Greek means 'story') were invented to explain how the world came to be and how we came to be in it. Myths were stories people told themselves in order to explain themselves to themselves and to others. But it was Aristotle who first developed this insight into a philosophical position when he argued, in his Poetics, that the art of storytelling – defined as the dramatic imitating and plotting of human action – is what gives us a shareable world.

It is, in short, only when haphazard happenings are transformed into story, and thus made memorable over time, that we become full agents of our history. This becoming historical involves a transition from the flux of events into a meaningful social or political community – what Aristotle and the Greeks called a polis. Without this transition from nature to narrative, from time suffered to time enacted and enunciated, it is debatable whether a merely biological life (zoe) could ever be considered a truly human one (bios). As the twentieth-century thinker Hannah Arendt argued: 'The chief characteristic of the specifically human life . . . is that it is always full of events which ultimately can be told as a story. . . . It is of this life, *bios*, as distinguished from mere *zoe*, that Aristotle said that it "somehow is a kind of action (*praxis*)".'[1]

What works at the level of communal history works also at the level of individual history. When someone asks you who you are, you tell your story. That is, you recount your present condition in the light of past memories and future anticipations. You interpret where you are now in terms of where you have come from and where you are going to. And so doing you give a sense of yourself as a *narrative* identity that perdures and coheres over a lifetime. This is what the German philosopher Dilthey called the coming-together-of-a-life (*Zusammenhang des Lebens*), meaning the act of coordinating an existence which would otherwise be scattered over time. In this way, storytelling may be said to *humanise* time by transforming it from an impersonal passing of fragmented moments into a pattern, a plot, a *mythos*.[2]

Every life is in search of a narrative. We all seek, willy-nilly, to introduce some kind of concord into the everyday discord and dispersal we find about us. We may, therefore, agree with the poet who described narrative as a stay against confusion. For the storytelling impulse is, and always has been, a desire for a certain 'unity of life'.[3] In our own postmodern era of fragmentation and fracture, I shall be arguing that narrative provides us with one of our most viable forms of identity – individual and communal.

If the need for stories has become acute in our contemporary culture, it has been recognised from the origin of time as an indispensable ingredient of any meaningful society. In fact, storytelling goes back over a million years, as scholars like

Kellogg and Scholes have shown. The narrative imperative has assumed many genres – myth, epic, sacred history, legend, saga, folktale, romance, allegory, confession, chronicle, satire, novel. And within each genre there are multiple sub-genres: oral and written, poetic and prosaic, historical and fictional. But no matter how distinct in style, voice or plot, every story shares the common function of *someone telling something to someone about something*. In each case there is a teller, a tale, something told about and a recipient of the tale. And it is this crucially intersubjective model of discourse which, I'll be claiming, marks narrative as a quintessentially *communicative* act. Even in the case of postmodern monologues like Beckett's *Krapp's Last Tape* or *Happy Days*, where the actor is talking and listening to him/herself, there is always at least an implicit other out there to whom the tale is addressed – that 'other' often being 'us' the listeners. In short, where the author or audience appear absent they are usually 'implied'. That is why the continuing, and I believe inexhaustible, practice of storytelling belies the faddish maxim that 'in narrative no one speaks', or worse, that language speaks only to itself.[4]

To imagine the origins of storytelling we need to tell ourselves a story. Someone, somewhere, sometime, took it into his head to utter the words 'once upon a time'; and, so doing, lit bonfires in the imaginations of his listeners. A tale was spun from bits and pieces of experience, linking past happenings with present ones and casting both into a dream of possibilities. Once the listeners heard the beginning they wanted to find out the middle and then go on to the end. Stories seemed to make some sense of time, of history, of their lives. Stories were gifts from the gods enabling mortals to fashion the world in their own image. And once the storytelling genie was out of the cave there was no going back. 'No one knows how long man has had speech', write Scholes and Kellogg in their classic book, *The Nature of Narrative*.

> Language is probably even older than man himself, having been invented by some 'missing link', a creature in the phylogenetic chain somewhere between man and the gibbon. It may have been as many as a million years ago that man first repeated an utterance which had given pleasure to himself or to someone else and thereby invented literature. In a sense, that was the beginning of Western narrative art.[5]

The magical power of narrative was not lost on its first hearers. And, as anthropologists like Lévi-Strauss and Mircea Eliade have shown, one of the earliest roles of the shaman or sage was to tell stories which provided symbolic solutions to contradictions which could not be solved empirically. In the process, reality itself would find itself miraculously transformed. The classic example, cited by Lévi-Strauss, is of the woman who has difficulties giving birth: suffering from a blocked womb, she is told the 'myth' of the good warriors freeing a prisoner trapped in a cave by monsters, and on hearing the plot resolution recited by the shaman, she gives birth to her child.[6] Thanks to an imaginary break-through, reality follows suit. Nature imitates narrative.

But stories served to address psychic as well as physical suffering. The pain of loss and confusion, of loved ones passing away, called out for stories.[7] Myths arose, as Lévi-Strauss says, as 'machines for the suppression of time'. Or as Tolkien put it, as ways of expressing our yearning for the Great Escape – from death. From the word go, stories were invented to fill the gaping hole within us, to assuage our fear and dread, to try to give answers to the great unanswerable questions of existence: Who are we? Where do we come from? Are we animal, human or divine? Strangers, gods or monsters? Are we born of one (mother-earth) or born of two (human parents)? Are we creatures of nature or culture? In seeking to provide responses to such unfathomable conundrums – both physical and metaphysical – the great tales and legends gave not only relief from everyday darkness but also pleasure and enchantment: the power to bring a hush to a room, a catch to the breath, a leap to the curious heart, with the simple words 'Once upon a time'.

We might thus account for the genesis of stories in so-called 'primitive societies'. But such powers of storytelling are not, I am convinced, as antiquarian as we might imagine. Just think how children today still crave for bedtime stories of fantastic creatures and conflicts – from Grimm's fairytales to Tolkien's Lord of the Rings – so that they may act out their inner confusions through these imaginary events and so, in the safety of their beds, prepare for sleep.[8] As Tolkien himself put it, describing his own childhood passion for stories:

> Fantasy, the making or glimpsing of Other-worlds, was the heart of the desire of Faerie. I desired dragons with a profound desire. Of course, I in my timid body did not wish to have them in the neighbourhood, intruding into my relatively safe world, in which it was, for instance, possible to read stories in peace of mind, free from fear.[9]

Are we adults so very different when it comes to the need for narrative fantasy?

The Greek term mythos meant, as noted, a traditional story. And in its earliest form, that is just what narrative was. Our modern question – where does narrative come from? – did not arise back then. The aim was not so much to invent something that never happened, or to record something that did happen, but to retell a story that had been told many times before. Primordial narratives were thus essentially *recreative*. And myth, the most common form of early narrative, was a traditional plot or storyline which could be transmitted from one generation of tellers to the next. It generally had a sacred ritual function, being recited for a community in order to recall their holy origins and ancestors. This is true of the great mythological sagas of Greek, Indian, Babylonian, Persian, Chinese, biblical, Celtic and Germanic traditions, to name but obvious cases. What would we know of Western cultural identity, more specifically, if we could not recite the tales of Odysseus, Aeneas, Abraham or Arthur, for example? And the same reliance on narrative recreation applies to non-Western cultures, as the Indian novelist Arundhati Roy reminds us. 'The Great Stories', she writes,

> are the ones you have heard and want to hear again. The ones you can enter anywhere and inhabit comfortably. They don't deceive you with thrills and trick endings. They don't surprise you with the unforeseen. They are as familiar as the house you live in. Or the smell of your lover's skin. You know how they end, yet you listen as though you don't. In the way that although you know that one day you will die, you live as though you won't. In the Great Stories you know who lives, who dies, who finds love, who doesn't. And yet you want to know again. THAT is their mystery and their magic.

But there is another mystery too. For every time that the Great Myths of Beginning are told, they are told by a *human* teller. So while they are the same, they are also just that little bit *different* at each telling. The storyteller 'tells stories of the gods, but his yarn is spun from the ungodly, human heart'.[10]

Mythic narrative mutated over time into two main branches: historical and fictional.

Historical narrative modified traditional *mythos* with a growing allegiance to the reality of past events. Storytellers like Herodotus and Thucydides in Greece, for instance, strove to describe natural rather than supernatural events, resisting the Homeric licence to entertain monstrous and fantastic scenarios. Alexander and the Persians took the place of Odysseus and the Sirens. The first historians strove to provide narrative descriptions of 'real' time, place and agency, making it seem as if they were telling us the way things *actually* happened. At the level of individual humans, this gave rise to the genre of biography or 'case history'. At the level of collective humanity, it gave birth to history in the general sense, understood as the narrative recounting of empirical events (*res gestae*).

The second branch of narrative, the *fictional*, also moved away from traditional *mythos*, but in a different direction from the historical. Fictional narratives aimed to redescribe events in terms of some ideal standard of beauty, goodness or nobility. This reached its most dramatic form in *romance*, a literary genre typified by such works as the *Chanson de Roland* and *Perceval*, where metaphor, allegory, hyperbole and other rhetorical devices served to embellish and embroider the events. But one already found strains of it in Dante's *Commedia*, where historical verisimilitude combined with fantasy and imagination, without losing sight of the basic human impulse to tell a story 'as if' it were happening, and 'as if' the characters described existed – or could be believed to exist.

It was, however, with the emergence of the modern *novel* in the post-Renaissance period that fictional romance reached its apogee. What differentiates the novel from preceding kinds of romance is its extraordinary 'synthetic' power: it draws liberally from such diverse conventions as *lyric* (personal voice), *drama* (presentation of action), *epic* (depiction of heroes or anti-heroes) and *chronicle* (description of empirical detail). But above all, the novel is unique in its audacity in experimenting and evolving, metamorphosing and mutating into an amazingly rich range of narrative possibilities – even entertaining the hypothesis of its own demise in what some commentators describe as anti-narrative or post-narrative. And as we enter the cyber-world of the third millennium where virtual reality and digital communications rule, we find many advocates of the apocalyptic view that we have reached the end not only of history, but of the story itself.

This pessimistic attitude towards our new cyber and media culture is canvassed curiously by critics of both the left (Benjamin, Barthes, Baudrillard) and the right (Bloom, Steiner, Henri). Their bottom line is that we are entering a civilisation of depthless simulation inimical to the art of storytelling. The exclusive vulgarisation of intimacy and privacy in popular culture – ranging from TV Talk Shows to multiple Chat Rooms on the Internet – appears to be exhausting the fundamental human need to say something meaningful in a narratively structured way. There is now, we are told, nothing that can't be immediately confessed to anonymous strangers 'somewhere out there', the most secret realms of experience being reducible to voyeuristic immediacy and transparency. Narrative is being superficialised and consumerised out of existence. And the fact that computers can now supposedly produce stories to order – as in the case of the Jacqueline Susann novel *Just this Once* – merely adds to the cynicism. The pseudo-Susann novel was written by a supercharged Apple-Mac computer called Hal, after the computer in 2001: *A Space Odyssey*, and published to a fanfare of publicity in 1993. But as even Professor Marvin Minsky, AI pioneer from MIT, admitted, no matter how many computer-coded rules you use to program your writing project, you still have to confront what he calls the 'common sense knowledge problem'. Computers can certainly copy and simulate, but the question remains whether they can *create* in a way comparable to a human narrative imagination.

A postmodern cult of parody and pastiche is, the pessimists conclude, fast replacing the poetic practices of narrative imagination. We shall see. For my part I am convinced that the obituarists of storytelling, be they positivists who dismiss it as anachronistic fantasy or post-structuralists who decry its alleged penchant for closure, are mistaken. Indeed, against such prophets of doom, I hold that the new technologies of virtualised and digitised imagining, far from eradicating narrative, may actually open up novel modes of storytelling quite inconceivable in our former cultures. One thinks, for example, of the way that Beckett explores the electronic retelling of one's life in *Krapp's Last Tape* (where a 69-year-old man rehears and retells the story of his 39-year-old former self through a tape-recorder); or, more graphically still, the way in which Atom Egoyan renarrates the Beckett play through the more sophisticated technologies of cinema and DVD. The complex narrative relationship between memory and recorded memory, between imagination and reality, can be brought into especially sharp focus by the new and technically avant-garde media. Moreover, this option is being fruitfully explored by a whole range of experimental film-makers from Chris Marker in *Level 5* (and his accompanying art work and CD-ROM, *Immemory*) to Tom Tykwer in *Run Lola Run*. That is why I believe that no matter how 'post' our third-millennium culture becomes, we shall never reach a moment when the phrase 'This is a story about . . .' ceases to fascinate and enchant. Hence my wager that postmodernism does not spell the end of the story but the opening up of alternative possibilities of narration.

But let me return briefly to our genealogy of storytelling. What both *historical* and *fictional* narratives have in common is a *mimetic* function. From Aristotle to Auerbach, it has been recognised that this involves far *more* than a mere mirroring of reality. When Aristotle defines *mimesis* in his *Poetics* as the 'imitation of an action', he means a creative redescription of the world such that hidden patterns and hitherto unexplored meanings can unfold. As such *mimesis* is essentially tied to *mythos* taken as the transformative plotting of scattered events into a new paradigm (what Paul Ricoeur calls the 'synthesis of the heterogeneous').[11] It has little or nothing to do with the old naturalist conviction that art simply holds a mirror up to nature.

Narrative thus assumes the double role of *mimesis-mythos* to offer us a newly imagined way of being in the world. And it is precisely by inviting us to see the world *otherwise* that we in turn experience *catharsis*: purgation of the emotions of pity and fear. For while narrative imagination enables us to empathise with those characters in the story who act and suffer, it also provides us with a certain aesthetic distance from which to view the events unfolding, thereby discerning 'the hidden cause of things'. It is this curious conflation of empathy and detachment which produces in us – viewers of Greek tragedy or readers of contemporary fiction – the double vision necessary for a journey beyond the closed ego towards other possibilities of being.

Aristotle confined this cathartic power to fictional and poetic narratives, maintaining that these alone revealed the 'universal' structures of existence – unlike historical accounts, which dealt merely with 'particular' facts. But I would wish to contest such a schismatic opposition and acknowledge some kind of interweaving between fiction and history. One of my main preoccupations in this book will be to explore various examples of such interweaving, and to unravel some of the more intriguing enigmas which result. In the chapters which follow, I shall endeavour to treat of a number of actual stories, before trying to sketch out a more precise philosophy of story-telling in our final section. I shall be returning, therefore, in conclusion to Aristotle and certain contemporary thinkers about narrative and would hope to be in a position at that point to offer a clearer conceptual account of the characteristics of storytelling. In other words, before getting to the moral of the story, I shall first engage with stories themselves. Before the theory the practice.

Hence, in what follows I propose first to explore the controversial relation between fiction and history in three individual cases – Stephen Daedalus, Ida Bauer (Dora) and Oscar Schindler. Then, I shall extend the discussion to three examples of more collective or national narration: Rome, Britain and America. By means of such examples – drawn from literature, cinema, art, psychotherapy and political history – my aim is ultimately to disclose a philosophical view instructed by the rich complexities and textures of these narratives. That way, we may not just be putting thinking into action but also, with luck, some action back into thinking.

In the light of these various explorations of narrative, sometimes probing the very limits of the sayable, I shall conclude that narrative *matters*. Whether as story or history or a mixture of both (for example testimony), the power of narrativity makes a crucial difference to our lives. Indeed, I shall go so far as to argue, rephrasing Socrates, that the unnarrated life is not worth living.

Part Two

Three Case Histories: Daedalus, Dora, Schindler

From History to Story:
The Case of Stephen Daedalus

Two

How to get the real into the made-up?
Ask me an easier one.

Seamus Heaney, **Electric Light**

ONE: JOYCE'S JOURNEY

Stephen Daedalus epitomises the fictional hero who wants to reinvent himself. Already in *A Portrait of the Artist as a Young Man*, Joyce's young protagonist vows to escape from the straitjacket of tradition and recreate himself in the 'silver womb of imagination'. To this end Stephen declares that he will not serve that in which he no longer believes, whether it call itself faith, family or fatherland. 'You talk to me of nationality, language and religion', he retorts; 'I will try to fly by these nets.' And so, crafting his own narrative voice and invoking his own namesake as 'fabulous artificer', Daedalus sets out in the final pages of the novel to 'forge in the smithy of his soul the uncreated conscience of his race'. In short, Stephen is adamant that it is not history which will write his story but his story which will rewrite history. Or as he brazenly boasts to his Dublin classmates, he will not be remembered because of Ireland; it is Ireland that will be remembered because of him!

In *Ulysses*, Joyce follows Stephen's journey as he struggles to awaken from the 'nightmare of history' into a world transmuted by imagination. Resolved to jettison the 'mothers of memory' which continue to paralyse him – motherland, mother tongue and mother Church – Stephen refuses to pray at his mother's deathbed, striking off on an odyssey which he believes will lead to new possibilities of self-invention. This involves, for Joyce's hero, not only a spiritual escape from colonial and ecclesiastical entropy but also the task of reworking the established conventions of Western literature. In the Hollis St. Maternity Hospital, for example, Joyce plays with parodic rewritings of the English literary heritage, comparing the embryonic evolution of Mrs Purefoy's baby with various stages of the narrative tradition, running from Beowolf to the modern realist novel. And in the National Library episode he focuses more specifically on the story of *Hamlet*. Stephen makes a point of turning the Ghost's 'remember me' – a summons to mimetic repetition and revenge – into a plea to be born anew, replacing ancestral memory with fictional creation. The play, completed by Shakespeare just a year after his own father's death, is reread by Stephen as a story which enabled Shakespeare to become a father in his own right (his son was called Hamnet): that is, to pass from the inherited habits of filiality to a more mature sense of paternity and authorship. Joyce himself, it appears, was experiencing just such a crisis of transition during the years he composed *Ulysses* (after the birth of his own son Georgio in Rome). But Joyce sees another kind of liberation at work here too – that of the writer who transcends the lures that keeps his soul captive: in Shakespeare's case the mimetic rivalries of Stratford; in Joyce's, the petty jealousies of his literary peers in Dublin. Stephen resolves to transform the dross of his Dublin life into a fictional leap of faith.[1]

In these two novels, amongst the most innovative in modern fiction, Joyce sets out to tell the story of Dublin as it has never been told before. What is at issue is a narrative miracle of transubstantiation where simple contingencies of everyday existence can be transmuted into narrative 'epiphanies'. A literary version of divine demiurgy. That, and nothing less, is what storytelling meant to Joyce.

Joyce achieved with his stories things that were impossible to him in life. Through the mediating personage of Stephen Dedalus (an amalgam of first Christian martyr and legendary Greek artist who designed the labyrinth), Joyce managed to turn the city that paralysed and banished him into a bustling cosmopolis of struggling souls. The nondescript figure who had actually rescued Joyce from a humiliating brawl in Grafton St. – 'a cuckolded Jew named Hunter' – is resurrected as one of the most beloved characters of twentieth-century fiction, Leopold Bloom. And it is this same Bloom who serves as surrogate father for Joyce's own fictional son, Stephen. In the story of Stephen and Bloom, Joyce performs a narrative synthesis between a whole series of legendary fathers and sons: Yahweh and Christ, King Hamlet and Prince Hamlet, Odysseus and Telemachus, Shakespeare and Hamnet, etc. Not to mention the novel's imaginary transposition of the split in Joyce himself between father and son – a problem which, as noted, greatly preoccupied him during the writing of *Ulysses* between 1906 and 1921. It is no accident that *Ulysses* begins with the annunciation of the 'father and the son idea'; or that it climaxes with Bloom and Stephen struggling (in vain) to recreate, over a cup of cocoa in Eccles St., some kind of communion between paternity and sonship – balancing the pull of historical memory with the impulse to forge the 'uncreated conscience' of the future.

One might even hazard a guess that Joyce crafted *Ulysses* as a story which might bring together the two rival narratives of Western culture generally, namely the Graeco-Roman and the Judaeo-Christian. This is a book where extremes meet in a way that they could not do in history. A *coincidentia oppositorum* which Joyce seems to suggest is conceivable only through narrative imagination.

This project reaches its apogee, however, not in the Ithaca encounter between Bloom and Stephen in Eccles St., but in Molly's final soliloquy. It is after all in Molly's rumbustious and irreverent sequel to the father–son search that the twin narrative traditions are eventually conflated. 'GreekJew is JewGreek. Woman's reason', muses Molly. Or as Joyce himself wrote to his friend Valéry Larbaud, 'Ithaca is sterile. Penelope has the last word.' Here historical recall is transmuted from the prison house of resentment and guilt ('agenbite of inwit') into the free-associating abandon of untrammelled reverie. Envy converts to equanimity. Memory becomes *mémoire*. History re-emerges, jubilant and revivified, as story. The atoning Spirit between Father and Son turns out to be, in the heel of the hunt, the genie of storytelling itself.

A final conjecture, therefore: if *Ulysses* is indeed one of the most daring works of contemporary fiction, it is also a story which cleverly transliterates Joyce's own biographical history – bearing out his avowal that it is 'a brave man would invent something that never happened!'. Such, perhaps, is the paradox of all great fiction.

TWO: REVIVALISTS AND MODERNISTS

Joyce was not the only writer of his culture to wrest fictional triumph from historical failure. Several of his compatriots also looked to storytelling as compensation for the mortifications of famine, disinheritance, poverty, priest-ridden philistinism, insular rivalry, loss of language and mass emigration. Most notable of these were revivalists like Yeats and Synge and modernists like Beckett.

Yeats rewrote many of the ancient Celtic dramas and promoted an 'Ireland the poets have imagined'. While Synge, for his part, composed a play called *The Playboy of the Western World*, where the hero, Christy Mahon, lies to a story-starved community that he has killed his father and then becomes 'a man by the power of [that] lie'.

Opting for the modernist trail, Beckett followed Joyce to Paris and pursued his exploration of the experimental resources of narrative – in both fiction and drama. Indeed, it is probably true to say that if Synge and Yeats pushed the romantic side of Stephen Daedalus's imagination to its logical extreme, transposing history by sheer fiat, Beckett probes the more postmodern proclivities of that imagination to the point where it poses vexing questions about its own condition of possibility. The long list of Beckettian vice-narrators, from Murphy and Moran to Molloy and Malone, never cease asking whether they should actually go on narrating or not. To tell or not to tell? becomes the recurring refrain of these tormented storytellers. How much of the past should we remember and how much reinvent? What is the difference, as Krapp asks, between literal and literary memory, between becoming a man by the power of a lie and becoming a madman? How do we balance (a) the poetic licence to recreate our past with (b) the involuntary recall of 'the suffering of being'? In short, is it ever really possible to weave a middle way between our opposing fidelities to story and history? Such are the quandaries assailing postmodern authors like Beckett.

Most fiction-writers, I believe, respond in one way or another to the double injunction of narrative – tell it, but do not tell it exactly as it was. This twofold exigency can be interpreted in different ways.

On the one hand, we have the Beckettian persuasion that since most forms of narrative are fibs to ward off the pain of the real, we should pare our stories down until they become 'residua' or 'no-texts'. (Such literary asceticism finds typical voice in Beckett's *Malone Dies* or *No's Knife*, texts of 'noman'.) This manoeuvre corresponds to what Maurice Blanchot – Beckett's French contemporary – called a 'writing of disaster' or 'demise literature': a sort of struggle between story and unstory (*non-récit*) which allows for posthumous voices to speak from their own 'wounded space'.[2] Here we find the narrator imagining, for example, that imagination is dead – but *still*, therefore, imagining. A performative contradiction perfectly captured in Beckett's own title: *Imagination Dead Imagine*. This is indeed storytelling in straits, but it is storytelling nonetheless.

On the other hand, we have the Joycean imperative to re-create history in its entirety, epitomised in the resolve to *tell everything so that nothing remains alien to what is told!* This latter signals an aesthetic of bold omnipotence at the opposite end of the spectrum to Beckett's self-confessed 'aesthetic of failure'. And most Anglo-Irish writing after them is, I would hold, inscribed somewhere in between.

THREE: DAEDALUS'S HERITAGE NOW

The legacy of Stephen Daedalus is alive and well in contemporary Irish fiction. A whole bevy of post-Joycean authors from Banville, Higgins and McGahern to Doyle, Johnston, Healy, Tobin, Carson and McLiam Wilson have continued the legacy of stories about stories, reflecting on the rich blend of narrative and reality that Joyce and Beckett made the staple diet of their writing. These writers share a common passion to explore the enigma of memory as recounted in fiction. Like Daedalus before them, they are fascinated by how history is altered in the telling, how the retelling itself changes the way things were in order to make a story out of how things *might have been*. (The future anterior is a favourite tense.) And they wonder how poetic lies, which ostensibly distort truth, can contrive at times to tell another kind of truth, sometimes a truer truth.

As I have addressed the question of Daedalus's literary descendants elsewhere,[3] suffice it to conclude here with a few brief samples which are emblematic, as I see it, of the basic narrative conundrum: namely, can fictional stories be true?

The first I take from Roddy Doyle's fictional account of the 1916 Rebellion, *A Star Called Henry*. Doyle retells the famous national uprising against the British through the story of a one-legged man who invents not only his name but his entire life. History, Doyle seems to be suggesting, is as subject to revisions and revampings as the case history of a particular individual – Henry Smart – who participated in it. 'Where was he and where did he come from?' asks his son, the book's narrator, who immediately confesses that he actually knows 'nothing real' about his father. He doesn't even know if his name was real, or the tales he told about his grandma and brothers and cousins, or about how he lost his leg. Was it amputated because of disease, stolen by the fairies, or lost when he was fighting the Zulus? Was Henry a butler to the Queen? A sailor who sailed the seas? A soldier who triumphed on the battle field? Or worse, a gambler, a peddler or a whore's bully? Was Henry even called Henry? 'He made his life up as he went along', the narrator-son admits. 'He left a trail of Henry Smarts before he finally disappeared.' This prompts the narrator to ask: 'Was he just a liar?' His answer: 'No, I don't think so. He was a survivor; his stories kept him going. Stories were the only things the poor owned. A poor man, he gave himself a lie. He filled the hole with many lives.'[4] The rewriting of the Irish national rebellion in Dublin in 1916 is thus performed through the mind of a fictional character who rewrites his own story.

Dermot Healy expresses a similar puzzlement in his novel *The Bend for Home* when he has his narrator wonder if writers 'to be memorable, dispense with accuracy'. The story, concerned with individual rather than political memory, is composed of multiple micro-stories which try to respond to this query. One such anecdote is that of the narrator's mother who took the fictional lines of a famous Percy French song as true. The popular ballad, 'Come Back Paddy Reilly to Ballyjamesduff', contains a verse about a taxi driver who used to collect the road engineer and balladeer, Percy French, from the railway station in the town of Ballyjamesduff until one day he went off to America. The ballad tells the story of Mr French trying to persuade the cabman, Paddy Reilly, to return, providing precise travel directions down to the last detail of where to 'turn left at the bridge of Finea' in order to make the final mile home. Now, as it happens, there is no such left turn in reality. Percy French abandoned the geographical accuracy of the engineer in order to get 'a couplet true'. He made the facts serve the story. In short, he needed the rhyme and reason of song, not reality. And who can blame him? It's called poetic licence. The liberty of every good storyteller. But there is more to it than that. By taking the fictional as true, the narrator's mother actually followed the directions given in the ballad and ended up at her desired destination! Fiction made possible what was impossible in reality. Or so the story says.

The narrator then goes on to explore how stories allow us to tell certain things about our lives which we would never allow ourselves to tell in real life. In fantasy, as it were, the guards are down, the censors gone on holiday, and all kinds of suppressed or silenced material can find its way into language for the first time. This is what I think Joyce was actually getting at when he made that rather shocking statement (at least to romantic ears) that we only invent that which has happened – or could have happened. This is how Healy's narrator puts it:

Can I lie here and side step some memory I'd rather not entertain, and then let fiction take care of it elsewhere, because that is sometimes what fiction does? It becomes the receptacle for those truths we would rather not allow into our tales of the self. The made-up characters feel their way by virtue of thoughts that novelists deny having.

But this does not mean, as might first appear, a collapsing of the distinction between the imaginary and the real. On the contrary, it is only made possible by this distinction. The imaginary liberates the prisoners of our lived experience into possible worlds where they may roam and express themselves freely, articulating things that generally dare not say their names and giving to our inexperienced experience the chance to be experienced at last. And though such experience is vicarious – i.e. unreal on the face of it – it is experience none-theless; and one *more* real sometimes than that permitted in so-called reality. Healy puts it well when describing his first attempt at writing about rain: 'I can still remember the liquid feel of those words for rain. How the beads were blown against a windowpane, and glistened there and ran. The words for rain were better than the rain itself.'[5]

If words for rain can do that to rain, what about words for love and pain and fear and shame and hope and the people who experience such things? This is, arguably, why we sometimes weep more freely – and get more deeply in touch with our grief – at narrative accounts or memories of a death than at the moment of the death itself. As in the story of the young widow who could not cry when confronted with her spouse's corpse – the pain being too great – but wept copious tears when she went to a movie a week later and saw the story of another young widow who could not cry when confronted with her spouse's corpse. . . . T. S. Eliot was quite right, I suspect, when he said that humankind cannot bear too much reality. For just as the body releases endorphins to cope with unbearable pain, so too the human psyche has all kinds of denial mechanisms against loss. But what is unpalatable and unspeakable in life is not so in fiction. As J. R. R. Tolkien put it, stories are 'prophylactic against loss' in a way which allows the loss to be articulated. And it is through the *quasi*-experience of loss, which fiction solicits, that we may even acquire a certain cathartic licence to reconnect with truths from which we were protected in everyday existence. Aristotle had already touched on this when he claimed that fictional *mimesis* can disclose essential truths of life closed off to the empirical historian. But Tolkien offers an even bolder version of the paradox:

> Probably every writer making a secondary world, a fantasy, every sub-creator . . . hopes that the peculiar qualities of this secondary world are derived from Reality, or are flowing into

it. . . . The peculiar quality of the 'joy' in successful Fantasy can thus be explained as a sudden glimpse of the underlying reality or truth. It is not only a 'consolation' for the sorrow of this world, but a satisfaction, and an answer to the question, 'Is it true?'[6]

Healy offers his own humorous version of the truth-in-fiction paradox when he goes on to recount how he achieved his first literary fame, like Synge's Playboy before him, 'by the power of a lie'. He describes returning to a wedding in his native Cavan after some months in exile in London. At the wedding reception he finds himself seated beside the editor of the local newspaper, the *Anglo-Celt*, in which he'd published his first short story some years previously. Asked by the editor how the writing was going for him in London, Healy made up a story about having finished a play that would soon be shown on British television. Responding to the editor's more detailed inquiries, Healy invented a further string of fibs – it was called *Nightcrossing*, he'd received an advance of one thousand pounds, and so on. The dancing started up then, and Healy forgot all about the play he'd never written. He returned to London a few days later, but his lie returned to haunt him. When he was seated in an Irish pub in Piccadilly a week after the wedding, another expatriate came in and clamped a copy of the most recent *Anglo-Celt* down on the bar. And there on the front page was the headline: 'CAVAN AUTHOR FINDS FAME'!

Healy had quite a job getting out of that fix. But it was precisely the story he made up about the play he'd never written which ultimately enabled him to write a play. Healy ended up becoming a fiction-writer, as it were, by the power of a fiction. Everything he wrote since, Healy admits, was an attempt to 'make up for that terrible lie. Had I not lied I might never have tried my hand at fiction. The truth is the lie you once told returning to haunt you'.[7]

I conclude with an extract from Robert McLiam Wilson's, *Eureka Street*, a novel which shows how the very humanity of people, and indeed of the places they inhabit, resides in the fact that they are carriers of stories. Cities like Belfast, where the novel unfolds, are revealed as 'meeting places of stories'. (A point also ingeniously explored by another Belfast writer, Ciaran Carson, in his recent *Fishing for Amber* and *Shamrock Tea*.) We read: 'The men and women there are narratives, endlessly complex and intriguing. The most humdrum of them constitutes a narrative that would defeat Tolstoy at his best and most voluminous.' The narrator's point seems to be that human lives embody narratives which no fictional narrative could ever accurately transpose. Novels impose some kind of selection and sequence on the Babel of stories, spoken and unspoken, that are jangled and jumbled together in a modern city. The city absorbs all of the narratives, past and present, into itself, like paper absorbing ink. And the citizens themselves cannot but write their lives onto this paper, even though their testimonies are for the most part 'involuntary'. In such a scenario, the novelist becomes someone who discloses rather than imposes, who listens gently when the city quietens and sleeps, so that he might 'hear the ghosts of stories whispered'. And at such times, the storyteller feels himself in the presence of something greater than himself.

In one especially haunting sequence of the book, the narrator recounts the stories of a number of victims of paramilitary assassination. And by giving them back their stories he gives history back to their lives. Refusing simply to count the cadavers and list the injuries, the author brings us inside their heads and skins. This is how he records the lost life of one such victim, a young man called Martin O'Hare:

> The young man who had opened the door for her – he was thirty-four but still had unlined skin and thick hair, had always been thought younger than he was but what had irritated him in his early twenties now delighted him, as he saw his old school friends married or bald and he could still comfortably date girls ten years younger than himself – was also killed, though he took nearly twenty seconds to stop existing. Some of the display case had removed one of his legs completely and mutilated his groin and pelvis. Glass from the door had smashed open his face, ripping off his nose, and penetrated his brain. His name was Martin O'Hare. He had been to school. He had read *Great Expectations* and had wanted to be an astronomer. He had been in love with people and people had been in love with him. He too had a story.[8]

The irony is, of course, that while *Eureka Street* insists that the stories of living people are so much more rich and complex than those found in novels, it is only because of novels like this that the 'involuntary' narratives of people like Martin O'Hare find a voice.

From our above discussion we might extrapolate three distinct, if often overlapping, senses of storytelling.

First, there are stories which we inherit from our family, culture or religion. These are the narratives of fatherlands and motherlands: ancestral stories which often function as *myths*. As such they can work as purveyors of tradition and heritage or of ideological illusion and cover-up. Or to put it in Joycean terms, they can serve as 'signatures of things' or as 'nightmares of history'.

Second, there are stories which serve the purpose of creation, in the sense of pure *creatio ex nihilo*. Here too we may encounter illusion and artifice, but in this instance we are responsible for it in so far as we are in the business of self-invention. It is in this sense that Stephen speaks of Daedalus, his namesake, as 'fabulous artificer' and determines to recast himself in the 'womb of imagination'.

Third, we have the sense of stories as creative solutions for actual problems. Here narrative fiction draws from the first two functions while adding a supplementary one – that of cathartic survival. An example of this might be Joyce's narrative task of transmuting the grist of everyday suffering into a sublimated work of art. In short, fiction as healing and transformative fantasy.

Whose Story is it Anyway? The Case of Dora
Three

While so far in Part 2 we have been dealing with fiction, when it comes to real life, the narrative impulse has very different repercussions. Here questions of how and what we recount have huge implications at both an existential and an ethical level.

If fiction is free to recreate the past *as it might have been* – operating with the diplomatic immunity of poetic licence – history has an obligation to recount the past *as it actually was*. By way of exploring the critical role narrative retelling plays in our actual lives, I shall first focus on the controversial 'case history' of Dora, which became something of a *cause célèbre* in Freudian psychotherapy.

ONE: THE TALKING CURE

For Freud, the 'talking cure' occurs when one gets to the bottom of things. The suffering subject strives to remember and recount the *whole story*, or at least as much of it as is recoverable given the lapses of time between the events of trauma and the recall of these events.

This was Freud's view in the controversial case of Ida Bauer, his young Jewish patient in Vienna otherwise known as Dora. Published in 1905 under the title 'Fragment of an Analysis of a Case of Hysteria', it soon became the most famous study of

31 **On** Stories

hysterical amnesia and narrative recovery.[1] Here Freud believed that he could cure his patient's symptoms if only he could reconstitute the 'missing pieces' in Dora's fragmented story. The story as presented was *prima facie* that Dora slapped Herr K., her father's close friend, after he made a pass at her on a walk one day. Dora's own father, who brought Dora to Freud for treatment after this event, was himself having an affair with Herr K.'s wife. Refusing to collude with the tacit exchange of women between Herr K. and her father, Dora struck out and refused Herr K.'s illicit advances. But this was not enough for Freud. There must, he was convinced, be something more, something hidden, some unconscious desire whose repression was resulting in Dora's illness. Freud's basic theory, enunciated in this case, was that hysterics suffer from blockages of memory which result in 'hysterical conversion symptoms' such as (in Dora's case) insomnia, depression, headaches, coughing fits and so on. The hypothesis was, accordingly, that Dora would recover physically once her repressed drives and traumas were symbolically recovered in and through narrative – that is, once she succeeded in telling her full story: her secret wish to marry Herr K., her father's friend. The therapy would therefore, Freud hoped, comprise a 'talking cure' made possible by the retrieval of repressed desire through analytic discourse and transference.

The same applied to Freud's other case histories – Little Hans, the Ratman, the Wolfman, Schneider – a telling concession being that the decisive evidence had to be revealed more as 'creative narrative' than as 'scientific fact'. Or as Freud himself put it in 'Constructions in Analysis', such constructed narrative 'can be inaccurate but sufficient'.[2] But there was an immediate problem here. How could one know whether narratives were 'true' or not? It was precisely the difficulty of responding to this question that provoked the controversy surrounding Freud's changing views on the seduction theory – at one time suggesting that childhood memories of abuse were *real*, at other times claiming that they were *fantasy*.

In fact, in a letter to Fliess after he abandoned his early 'realist' claims for the seduction theory, Freud argued that it was ultimately impossible to distinguish between truth and fiction in narratives deriving from the unconscious. Indeed, it was Freud's ostensible move away from the real world to that of fantasy that prompted critics like Elaine Showalter and Jeffrey Masson to describe the psychoanalytic movement as an 'assault on truth'. In short, memories ceased to be treated as traces of empirical abuse and were treated more as fanciful imaginings or as responses to the therapist's own suggestions, hints and guesses; a view echoed in Freud's claim that we should attend less to the 'assertions of the patients themselves' than to the emerging story of the unconscious. Serve the story and the symptoms will dissolve.

This provokes Showalter to argue that Freud forced such reminiscences on his patients, 'eliciting confabulations rather than actual memories'. Speaking of Freud's specific approach to the case of Dora, she writes:

> Committed from the start to the hysteria diagnosis, he interpreted all Dora's behaviour and statements in accordance with his theories. He told her that she was really attracted to Herr K., in love with her father, and with Freud himself. He ignored the appalling circumstances of Dora's family situation, and after only eleven weeks she broke off the therapy.[3]

Jeffrey Masson is even more blunt in his accusation that

'[Dora] felt lied to. She was lied to. She felt used. She was used.'[4]

I don't propose to rehearse the history of this controversy here. Suffice it to say that from an ethical and juridical stand-point (never mind the complex epistemological issues of how we can ever *know* the past as past), it *does* and *should* matter whether a recovered memory relates to things which actually happened. And this mattering pertains both to the person allegedly abused and to the person who allegedly perpetrated the abuse.

TWO: FALSE MEMORY SYNDROME

We have seen recently, particularly in the United States, a wide debate on the so-called 'false memory syndrome'. This has been documented in a number of highly publicised books, for example Michael Yapko's *Suggestions of Abuse: True and False Memories of Childhood Sexual Trauma*, Lenore Terr's *Unchained Memories: True Stories of Traumatic Memories*, Lawrence Wright's *Remembering Satan*, Mark Prendergast's *Victims of Memory* and, perhaps most controversial of all, Frederick Crewes's (ed.) *The Memory Wars*.[5] Though few of these contest the validity of 'persistent' memory of infantile trauma, several cast doubt on the use of 'suggestion' and 'trancework' techniques in cases of 'long-term recovered memory'. One frequently cited case is that of Mr Paul Ingram, accused by his daughter of perform-ing sexual abuse rites. The accusation was made after the plaintiff allegedly recovered a long repressed memory thanks to (1) her reading of literature on satanic rituals and (2) a number of trancework sessions with 'abuse experts'. The accused himself confessed to the crimes after sustained inter-rogations by police and psychologists, during which he was assured that the more he acknowledged the abuse the more clearly his own (repressed) memories of such events would be recovered. As Paul Ingram eventually compelled himself to admit, 'My memory is becoming clearer as I go through all this. . . . It's getting clearer as more things come out.' The basic 'suggestibility' premise of the interrogators was this: if you have the *feeling* that such abuse occurred, even if not a cognitive awareness, then it *did* occur. Mr Ingram was condemned to twenty years of imprisonment before the case was contested and reopened. (One could cite more notorious cases of such suggestion-confessions running from the Salem witch trials, dramatically captured in Arthur Miller's *The Crucible*, to the investigations of alleged satanic abuse of children in the Orkney Islands off Scotland in the 1990s.)

As a result of certain abuses of the memory of abuse (even if they be exceptions rather than the rule), the very notion of psychological memory is being threatened.[6] The undermining of testimonial narrative in this manner does a grave disservice not only to those falsely accused of abuse but also to those many victims of actual abuse. The *veracity* of stories of childhood abuse – recovered or persistent – is of capital importance (especially, I repeat, from a moral-judicial point of view).

Let me return for a moment to the case of Dora. The possibility of 'suggestion' is far from absent in this vexed case history – which itself comprises a history of revision and controversy. As several of Freud's successors noted, the 'talking cure' did not actually work for Dora for the probable reason that Freud construed her story according to his own unconscious identifications – in particular with the virile Herr K., whom Freud believed Dora secretly wished to marry. Freud's remarks about Dora's resistance to his hypothetical interpretation of her symptoms may thus betray a *counter-transference* of his own desires onto his analysand – a psychoanalytic phenomenon which Freud himself had not yet come to appreciate. But Freud did, in fairness, have the professional honesty to call this case history a 'fragment', thereby implicitly acknowledging that the 'missing pieces' of Dora's story were never fully filled in or completed by Dora herself.

The question raised by this fragmentary narrative is therefore: *whose story is it anyway?* Dora's or Freud's? Certain commentators, most notably Claire Kahane in *In Dora's Case*, read the oblique, truncated and unfinished character of Dora's story as a signal of its authenticity. Hysteria, this argument goes, is by its very nature an experience of fragmentariness; and its truthfulness derives from its uncompromising resistance to attempts by omnipotent father-figures to 'fill in' the fissures of the story in order to sign off a 'total account'. Dora's narrative has thus become in certain feminist circles a *cause célèbre* of feminine resistance – hysterical or otherwise – to the phallocentric demand to 'tell everything'. According to this view, it is precisely the cryptic, elusive and obscure elements in Dora's own version of events which constitute a necessary female refuge from the male imperative to know and appropriate everything alien to it.

THREE: THERAPY – BETWEEN STORY AND HISTORY

This reading is persuasively developed by Jane Gallop, who argues that hysterical discourse is a paradigm of 'woman's story' to be celebrated, not debunked. And it is also invoked by Stephen Marcus in his literary-psychological account 'Freud and Dora: Story, History, Case History', where he cites Dora's story as an exemplary instance of modernist fiction, displaying four of its central features: (1) the impossibility of access to truth; (2) the dissolution of linear narration and its explosion into multiple, often competing, perspectives; (3) the existence of an unreliable narrator (Freud); and (4) the undecidable relation between fiction and reality, both inside and outside discourse.[7]

What Marcus and some other commentators seem to ignore, however, is that if it is true that on an *aesthetic* level it matters little whether there is an accurate correspondence between narrative and reality, it matters hugely on an *ethical* level. It certainly mattered to Dora – who got worse rather than better thanks to Freud's counter-transferential account; and it matters to the many victims of real abuse before and after her. What is good for modernist or postmodernist fiction is not necessarily good for life. There is, after all, a need to discriminate, as best we can, between the pure *story-element* of case histories and the *history-element* referring to the past 'as it actually happened'.

The two strands – fiction and fact – are, admittedly, almost always interwoven in the narrative text; but that does not mean that the strands can never be, at least partially, disentangled and distinguished. Consequently, while I would not for a moment deny that literary analogies between Freudian case histories and modernist fiction can teach us much about the subtle and sophisticated uses of narrative (oral or written), such analogies do not do justice to the ethical significance of stories of *real* suffering – stories which the sufferers wish to be *recognised as true*, that is, as referring to events which *did* happen. Nobody suffering from real childhood trauma wants to be told, on going to an analyst, that he or she has the gift of a wonderful imagination.

One goes to therapy for relief of pain, not for lessons in creative writing.

I do not wish to deny, of course, that narrative plays a crucial role in the 'talking cure'. There are powerful arguments, as we shall see, in favour of a narrative approach to therapy which responds to the truth of suffering. In short, stories can sometimes retrieve psychic trauma in a way that more literalist diagnostic approaches cannot. Not all narratives follow the literary prerogative of suspending reference to reality in the name of pure fiction.

A good example of how narratives may be used in positive therapeutic fashion is offered by the psychiatrist Dr Robert Scholes, in his book *The Call of Stories: Teaching and the Moral Imagination*. The author here describes two different ways of approaching a 'patient' which, I believe, have an interesting bearing on the Dora case. The first involves a standard psychiatric categorisation of a certain woman patient as an 'untreatable phobic'. This routine medical procedure seeks to 'get a fix' on the patient by ascertaining what 'factors' or 'variables' are at work so as to make an 'objective diagnosis', present an 'abstract' and develop a 'therapeutic agenda'. The second approach begins by telling her story. Or to be more exact, by inviting her to tell *her* story so that when her analyst later tries to reach some understanding of her deep-rooted fears, often in consultation with fellow analysts, he does so in the knowledge that he is retelling her story. In this 'narrative' context the patient is humanised and given a history and a name; she becomes someone whose habit of being paralysed by various anxieties in her daily existence is part of a larger story involving childhood, schooling, desires, fascinations, friends, the kinds of clothes she wore, books she read and TV programmes she watched, where she travelled, how she met and married her husband, what kind of god or values she believed in, and so on. In short, the second approach acknowledges that behind every 'clinical history' lies a life-story. It recognises that behind every 'phobic', 'depressive', 'hysteric' and 'psychotic' there lies a person with a unique set of memories and circumstances. It promotes this manifesto for psychoanalysts: 'The people who come to see us bring us their stories. They hope they tell them well enough so that we understand the truth of their lives. They hope we know how to interpret their stories correctly. We have to remember that what we hear is their story.'[8]

A crucial point about these two approaches is not just that the latter is more humanising, but that it is also more effective. People suffering from psychiatric or psychological disorders are more likely to get better when they believe that their stories are being heard in addition to being 'treated' in a purely clinical or biochemical way. The difference between speaking of someone as (1) a textbook symptom of calculable causes or (2) a singular life in quest of narrative is not a matter of either/or. The good analyst, as Lévi-Strauss once noted, is both a 'scientist' who takes facts seriously and a 'shaman' who knows how to receive and tell stories. It is not enough to see sufferers as problems to be formulated; it is equally important to listen to them as a history of stories to be told. This means letting each patient be a teacher as well as a 'case'. Or as Coles puts it,

> Hearing themselves teach you, through their narration, the
> patients will learn the lessons a good instructor learns only
> when he becomes a willing student, eager to be taught . . .
> [when he] becomes a good listener in the special way a story

requires: noting the manner of presentation; the development of plot, character, the addition of new dramatic sequences; the emphasis accorded to one figure or another in the recital; and the degree of enthusiasm, of coherence, the narrator gives to his or her account.[9]

The problem with Dora's case may well be that it was treated by Freud less as a life in search of a history than as a (case) history in search of a life. That is, Freud may have been so persuaded by his own psychodynamic 'theory' of hysteria – in terms of repressed memories of Oedipal seduction and subsequent conversion symptoms – that he needed Dora's story to fit into the pre-scripted plot of his own 'case history'. Not that Freud could be accused here of the kind of egregious error committed in the infamous case of Emma Eckstein (when he misdiagnosed his patient as 'bleeding for love' of himself, when in fact she was haemorrhaging from a strip of gauze mistakenly left inside her nose after his friend Dr Fliess had performed an operation to cure an alleged 'nasal reflex neurosis'). He was clearly confused, however, as to whose story he was telling in both cases – his own or his patient's.

But while some critics read Freud's interpretative errors as a symptom of excessive scientism (reducing Dora or Emma to some theoretical model of cause and effect), others trace his own diagnoses to an excess of narrative imagination. Frank Cioffi, for example, is someone who claims that Freud was not scientific enough, abandoning the rigours of clinical medicine for literary fantasies. Freud approached his patient's dreams and reminiscences, according to Cioffi, 'more as a painter to his pigments than as a sleuth to his traces of mud and cigar ash'. The result being that instead of construing symptoms in terms of deterministic psychic mechanisms, he treated them as pretexts for the 'construction of associative chains to pre-selected termini', that is, as recipes for 'working a piece of fancy'.[10] And Frederick Crewes offers a no less damning verdict in his polemical introduction to *The Memory Wars*: 'the deviser of psychoanalysis was at bottom a visionary but endlessly calculating artist, engaged in casting himself as the hero of a multivolume fictional opus that is part epic, part detective story, and part satire on human self-interestedness and animality'.[11]

My own view is that the early Freud took himself too seriously as a medical rationalist – in order to find acceptance with the scientific establishment of his day. He was thus, I believe, initially reluctant to recognise that psychoanalysis was in significant measure a process of narrative transference and projection – and precisely *because* of that, one in great need of *critical and ethical discriminations*: discriminations which Freud and some of his followers seemed unwilling or ill-equipped to perform. In short, one of the biggest dangers for psycho-analysis, exposed by the Dora case, was therapy's insufficient awareness of its own narrative processes as it sought to unravel and negotiate an extremely sophisticated and unconscious web of history and story. It was, I suspect, because Freud often paid *too little* attention to his own story-telling impulses that he, and some of his patients, fell captive to them.

It is undeniable, when all is said and done, that Freud was genuinely moved by Dora's torments and inflammations, and kept returning to her case with almost obsessive concern. But the suspicion must remain that Dora did not get well because Freud was reading his own hypothesis into her life-story – projecting and counter-transferring his own paternal fantasy onto her supposed love for her father (and, by implication, for Herr K., and for Freud himself). The danger of psychoanalytic explanation is that what it ultimately tells us is itself. The story it narrates, under the guise of objective 'case history', is in fact its own autobiography writ large. Perhaps Freud himself was close to admitting as much when he conceded, on one occasion, that analytic interpretations might have as much to do with 'narrative' as with 'fact'. But, if so, more is the pity that Freud did not see the Dora case as the occasion to remind psychiatric medicine that the suffering human psyche is not only an assemblage of symptomatic data to be fitted into this or that clinical category, but also a history of unique stories – stories which compete with each other to make some kind of sense in terms of character, plot, reversal, transition and, above all, catharsis.

FOUR: A NARRATIVE PATH – BETWEEN RELATIVISM AND POSITIVISM

Several analysts who came after Freud did admit as much and took the narrativist approach further than the founder of psychoanalysis would have dreamed. Advocates of a more 'literary' psychoanalysis – such as Malcolm Bowie, Christopher Bollas and Adam Phillips – compare analysts to dramatists, novelists, fabulists or musicians, whose purpose is to evoke rather than inform. Certain neo-Lacanians, for their part, celebrate the virtues of analytic sessions as open-ended narratives where the analyst, no less than the analysand, has no fixed idea of denouement, thereby refusing traditional conventions of closure. Here the purpose is not to produce an 'exemplary story' that ties everything into a neat resolution but to undo this addiction to narrative closure. Analysis, on this count, works to free our pre-established history into multiple stories with various beginnings and middles – the more the merrier – and no final ends. 'There are no cures', as Phillips puts it, 'only ways of talking'.[12]

Certain practitioners of this narrative model, however, push it to what I would regard as relativist extremes. One such, in my view, is the constructivist R. Schafer, who argues that it does not matter what story is told as long as it *works*. Operating with loosely aesthetic and pragmatic criteria, he implies that there is nothing in past events themselves which compels us to interpret them in this manner rather than that. There is no real way of establishing the 'historical truth' of someone's life; so all we have is some kind of 'narrative truth' which fits the particular bill of this particular person at this particular time. What matters is that one tells a story and that someone (the analyst) *believes* this story so that 'therapeutic benefits' result. On this account, therefore, it is not possible to tell whether one narrative is any *truer* than another, only whether it is *better* than another, to wit, *more effective*. And therapeutic efficacy is in turn deemed to rest on the capacity of the analyst to persuade the patient that one version of the story is best (because more likely to 'work' for the patient). For such constructivists, extra-linguistic criteria of reference or veracity are totally subordinate to those of textual composition and preference. There is no question of the narrative being faithful to some allegedly independent reality. The therapy serves the story and the story serves the therapy.[13]

Certain statements in Freud himself, it could be argued, precipitated such a relativist turn; for example, when he warned that the simple excavation of conscious speech for unconscious memories does not follow a *correspondence* model of verification, but rather unveils a whole palimpsest of protective 'screen memories' – memories which, he showed, themselves involve a network of deeply camouflaged traumas and desires. We may never, Freud once admitted, discover a single 'kernel' to the plot which makes sense of the multiple sub-plots and side-stories. On the contrary, like many a modernist or postmodernist novel, the buried life of the psyche may itself rely upon unreliable narrators and unresolved plots. Dora's most truthful story, on this reading, would be closer to a Calvino or Beckett novel than a nineteenth-century realist classic by Hardy or Thackeray. And Freud would be guilty less of scientism than of fictionalism.

The psychoanalytic approach to screen memory often treats evidence more like a dream-to-be-interpreted (in different ways) than some archival fact to be uncovered. By establishing the disguise strategy of dream as paradigm of screen memory, psychoanalysis seems to be departing from the realist notion of remembrance as representation (the old correspondence theory). Abandoning his early 'scientific' idioms of causal thermodynamics, medical neurology and even archaeological excavation (leading back to a bedrock of empirical experience), Freud now appeared to be opting for more 'literary' idioms of remembrance, e.g. a 'mystic writing pad', simultaneously preserving and erasing traces of experience – an intertextual play of endlessly receding memories whose literal 'origin' is as debatable as it is invisible ('A Note Upon the "Mystic Writing Pad"', 1924). By the end of his life, Freud was actually questioning whether we have any reliable memories at all of our childhood (as it really happened) or just 'memories *relating* to our childhood'.[14] Memories were being increasingly read by him as 'dream books' inscribed with fears and anxieties which called out to be decoded and translated into new forms of retelling. It was less the story which enabled sufferers to find a cure than the very *telling* of it that suggested we were cured. Or as Freud's dissident disciple Ferenczi put it, 'the patient is not cured by free-associating, he is cured when he can free-associate'.

On this view, therapeutic accounts did not claim to *re-present* some real moment of the forgotten past so much as to release us from the illusion that any such 'literal' moment could ever be recaptured. Talk, it sometimes seemed, was enough in itself to emancipate the past into future possibilities.

FIVE: CONCLUSION

So how are we to negotiate the differences outlined above? A good use of narrative therapy might, I suggest, be thought of as one which transforms binding stories into freer ones, emancipating us from the straitjacket of solipsistic fancy. The important point to note here is that while we tell our life-stories to other people, or write them by ourselves for other people, there is no common genre of telling one's life-story *to oneself alone*.[15] Even Augustine's confessions were addressed to God, and Rousseau's confessions to fellow wounded narcissists! It takes two to story.

The analyst seeks to help sufferers by encouraging them to de-program their old histories, to divest themselves of the habitual plot-lines which have determined their behaviour up to now, and to reopen their life-stories to the gift of unpredictability, to surprise, to grace. Such rewriting, co-authored as it were by analyst and analysand, is what ultimately releases us from the pain and paralysis of repetition compulsion. In good therapy, it requires both a talker and a listener to retell a life-story. And good life-stories are those which can be retold in different ways.

I think that we can summarise the legacy of Dora's case – and other controversies surrounding the therapeutic role of narrative recall – in terms of three main models of readings. First, there is the 'scientistic' hypothesis of the early Freud and certain positivists, who hold that analysis is a way of neutrally observing the hidden 'facts' which originally 'caused' the patient's malady. This approach underestimates, I believe, the crucial role of narrative in therapy. Second, there is the 'relativist' hypothesis, sometimes hinted at by the later Freud and ultra-constructivists, who argue that the talking cure has less to do with recovering 'the past as it really was' than with loosening the unconscious into a free play of purely linguistic signifiers and fantasies. But this approach, as I have been suggesting, tends to ignore the irreducible (if highly complex) 'referential' dimension of analytic discourse. And finally, there is the more balanced and, I think, judicious approach of what I would call (after Ricoeur) the 'hermeneutic' hypothesis – namely, the view that the retelling of the past is an interweaving of past events with present readings of those events in the light of our continuing existential story.[16] This third approach requires that narrative *works* for us in the present as well as being *as true as possible* to the sufferer's own past. It is both therapeutic and referential in its claims, and the wiser for it.

Testifying to History: The Case of Schindler
Four

Since then, at an uncertain hour,
that agony returns;
And till my ghastly tale is told,
this heart within me burns.

Coleridge, **The Rime of the Ancient Mariner**

If questions of narrative truth are, as I've been arguing, crucial for individual cases of trauma, they are even more so when it comes to historical trauma. The instances of negationism with respect to the Holocaust and other genocides in history are timely reminders of the stakes involved. This is brought home to us each time we hear of Holocaust deniers receiving large fees and audiences at major university campuses, or revisionists like Nolde or Hillgruber in the German History Debates declaring that if it is true that the Jews suffered under the Nazis, it must be recalled that the Nazis suffered similarly under the Soviets.[1] In other words, it all depends who is telling the story. In such instances, the very credibility of memory as historical witness is at issue.

While revisionist historians like Maurice Faurisson and David Irving deny the existence of gas chambers, anti-revisionist historians like Lawrence Langer demonstrate just how fragile and indispensable the role of testimonial memory is. Indeed, in his extraordinarily moving book, *Holocaust Testimonies*, Langer's scrupulous distinctions between 'deep memory' and other variant categories of remembering –

'anguished', 'humiliated', 'tainted' and 'unheroic' – represent just the kind of typological work that is needed to answer those who would discredit the legitimacy of remembrance altogether. In this chapter, I want to explore the critical role of narrative in the historical memory of the Holocaust, taking as one of my primary examples the controversial story of 'Schindler's Jews'.

The first-hand narratives of Langer's work, no less than the literary witness of writers like Primo Levi, Elie Wiesel or, at fictional remove, Thomas Keneally in *Schindler's Ark*, serve to show just how essential narration is for the ethical remembrance of genocide. For Primo Levi, the need to recount his memoirs was a duty to have others participate in the events which might otherwise be forgotten, and by being forgotten, repeat themselves. For Wiesel, the reason he tells and retells the story is to give the victims 'the voice that was denied them' by history. Or as one of his characters puts it, searching for a Holocaust survivor in a New York psychiatric hospital: 'Perhaps it is not given to humans to efface evil, but they may become the consciousness of evil.' Recounting is a way of becoming such an ethical consciousness. For just as the Greeks knew that virtues were best transmitted by a retelling of the admirable deeds of heroes – the courage of Achilles, the constancy of Penelope, the wisdom of Teiresias, etc. – so too the horror of moral evil must be retrieved from oblivion by means of narrative remembering.[2] Keneally's historical novel of Oscar Schindler's rescue of Jews, later turned into a successful film by Steven Spielberg, is an attempt at such moral retrieval. But the matter, as we shall see, is far from simple.

Wiesel and other first-hand witnesses of the Shoah make an

important distinction between verbal and visual narratives of testimony. Not mentioning any specific films or images, Wiesel writes: 'Why this determination to show "everything" in pictures? A word, a glance, silence itself communicates more and better . . . the Holocaust is not a subject like all others. It imposes certain limits.'[3] What are these limits? It is hard to deny, for a start, that some of the Holocaust memorials have become forms of spectacle and kitsch without taste or sensitivity. The spectrum of images ranges from hyper-realist exhibits of gas chambers, ovens, mounds of bodies, emaciated children and barbed-wire fences to sensationalised Hollywood soap operas like Holocaust or controversial comic-strips like Maus by Art Spiegelman. It is understandable, in this context, that first-hand witnesses like Wiesel might rail against the 'merchants of images who set themselves up to speak for the victims'.[4] But one wonders if they are correct to see this as reason to question the validity of narrative testimony itself. 'Was it not a mistake to testify', asks Wiesel, 'and by that very act affirm their faith in man and word?'[5]

There is, I suggest, a delicate balance between the need (a) to use narrative imagination to revisit trauma and allow for a healing-mourning process and (b) to respect the unspeakable evil of that trauma. This immediately raises crucial issues about how to commemorate the Shoah without betraying it. How to represent without distorting? How, in dealing with the politics of memory, do we obviate the iniquity of oblivion on the one hand, and what Levi calls the facility of compulsory public distress on the other? The Holocaust, it seems true to say, has suffered from both under-remembrance and over-remembrance. The challenge is to remember in the right way.

In view of such scruples, Stephen Feinstein concludes his essay on *Witness and Legacy*, a major multi-media exhibition of Holocaust images, with a plea for the continuation of narrative memory: 'There is more and more of a burden and an increasing urgency to tell the story. The generation of witnesses is passing. All that will be left is the legacy. Throughout history, art has been a means of such telling. Within the realm of art, the Holocaust era may just be emerging.'[6]

ONE: SCREENING THE HOLOCAUST – THE SPIELBERG–LANZMANN CONTROVERSY

Similar scruples arise in connection with cinematic narrations of the Holocaust, though here the tensions between ethical and aesthetic fidelities to historical memory have proved more evident. I am thinking particularly of the controversy surrounding Spielberg's cinematic portrayal of the life of Schindler and the Jews he rescued from death camps in 1943. In a hard-hitting essay entitled 'Holocaust: The Impossible Representation' (1994), Claude Lanzmann – himself the maker of a documentary about the Holocaust, *Shoah* – delivered a blistering critique of Spielberg's attempt to transpose the 'irrepresentable' event of Auschwitz into dramatised images. According to Lanzmann, *Schindler's List* is guilty of a distortion of historical truth, for in this fictional recreation of the Holocaust everyone communicates with everyone, even the Jewish victims with their Nazi persecutors; whereas in reality Auschwitz was the absence of human language par excellence. By contrast, writes Lanzmann, *Shoah* is a film in which 'nobody meets anybody'; and he adds that this is for him an 'ethical position'. Lanzmann's quarrel is not with Spielberg's respect for 'historical detail' *per se*, or indeed with Thomas Keneally, who wrote the book on which the film is based. He fully respects the integrity of their intentions in this regard. His quarrel is with the manner in which such details and facts are *portrayed* – that is, *represented through narrative*. For Lanzmann, *Schindler's List* is a 'kitsch melodrama' which trivialises the unique character of the Holocaust. It transgresses by fictionalising it.

To extend this reading, the story of Schindler has been said to resemble other emotive depictions of the event such as *Life is Beautiful* or Caviani's *Night Porter* (where the relation of German and Jew is portrayed as a sado-masochistic psychodrama). Or, it has been deemed symptomatic of a more general tendency to portray the Shoah as an entertainment spectacle. One Holocaust museum in St Petersburg, Florida, for example, which is listed as number 11 in the local catalogue of '40 Fun Things to Do', offers 'genuine railway spikes from Treblinka' at cut-rate prices and scale-model replicas of the Polish boxcars that transported Jews to the camps at $39.95. And, surprisingly, this tendency to banalise horror by turning it into a spectator sport is not even entirely absent from the Wiesenthal Center's Museum of Tolerance in Los Angeles, whose publicity materials include 'special bonuses and group discounts' for the show, comprising 'high-tech, hands-on experiential . . . unique interactive exhibits' and 'biographies of children caught in the horrors of the Holocaust' which are 'updated daily'. This traducing of the Shoah has, some claim, even spread to the academic industry with the rise of agenda-setting Holocaust studies programmes, featuring such topics as 'An Afrocentric Critique of the Diary of Anne Frank' or 'The Holocaust and Femicide'. This slotting of the Shoah into a new culture of 'victimisation' studies, alongside gay and lesbian studies, disability studies, women's studies, etc. is arguably doing less to honour the memory of the dead than to 'turn the Holocaust into grist for the mill of academic trendiness or into a carnival'.[7]

Auschwitz prohibits representation through images, Lanzmann argues, not just for biblical reasons ('Thou shalt have no graven images'), but for moral reasons. To present the Shoah as spectacle is to invite voyeurism and *Schadenfreude*. To portray the death camps in terms of Hollywood psychodrama is to indulge in the unseemly frisson of vicarious abjection. Lanzmann is uncompromising:

> The Holocaust is first and foremost unique in that it builds around itself, in a circle of flames, the limit not to be crossed, because a certain absolute of horror is incommunicable: to pretend crossing it is to become guilty of the most serious transgression. Fiction is a transgression, I feel deeply that there is a prohibition of representation.

In short, while Spielberg offers an 'illustrated *Shoah*' where we, the spectators, are invited to participate emotionally in the story and identify with the hero (Schindler) and the victims (the Jews), Lanzmann refuses all dramatisation. Spielberg puts images where there are none in *Shoah*, concludes Lanzmann, and 'images kill imagination'.[8]

But what kind of 'imagination' are we talking of here? A *narrative* imagination, to be sure – the many real-life survivors who bear witness in the eight-and-a-half-hour running time of *Shoah* do so in terms of to-camera *testimonies*; but it is narrative with a difference. The witnesses speak not for themselves, not in the first person, but for others, for those who have been deprived of a voice. None of the survivors says 'I'; none tells a personal story, like those of 'Schindler's Jews'. Even the hair-cutter who survived Treblinka after three months of captivity does not explain how he did it. It is not that which interests him (the first-hand narrator), or indeed Lanzmann (the second-hand narrator). What matters is the voice of the voiceless, the remembering of what has been forgotten precisely as forgotten. The haircutter says 'we'. He is a voice speaking for the dead. In contrast to Spielberg, who, in Lanzmann's view, portrays the extermination as a backdrop to the heroic feat of Schindler, Lanzmann himself seeks to confront the 'blinding black sun' of the Holocaust: that blind spot of horror and evil which can never be adequately conveyed by conventional 'comparative' or 'comforting' identifications. There is no consolation in the broken narratives of *Shoah*. There are no tears to feel with, no sensations to orient oneself, no ecstasy, no catharsis, no purgation. There is, as Lanzmann admits, 'no possibility of crying'. By refusing the temptation of a redemptive or reconciliatory conclusion – like that of *Schindler's List* – Lanzmann opts for a form of narrative memory which testifies, first and last, to the need to remember our own forgetfulness.

How does he do this? By showing us witnesses who testify to the impossibility of representing what happened in Auschwitz, by letting a faltering voice or broken anecdote betray what no shot (fictional or documentary) of dead bodies could tell us. Namely, the impossibility of representing in images what these survivors saw with their own eyes. As J.-F. Lyotard puts it,

> *Shoah* resists the use of representation in images and
> music . . . and hardly offers a single testimony where the
> unrepresentable character of the extermination is not
> indicated, even momentarily, by the alteration of voice, a
> tightening of throat, a tear, a sob, the disparition of a witness

> out of frame, an upset in the tone of the narrative, some
> uncontrolled gesture.[9]

There is, quite literally, no way in which this past can ever be relived as a compensating presence. What is required here is narrative memory *without images*. Remembrance *without representation*. Communication of the incommunicable *without communion*.

Lawrence Langer makes a further point in *Holocaust Memories*, when he argues that the survivors' search for lost time is not conducted according to the Proustian manner of recovery, because the past they uncover 'does not fall into an intricate pattern illuminating the present but stops at the remembered disorder as if it were an insurmountable barrier'.[10] Survivors can bear witness only to what he calls 'insulated moments' which seem to have been preserved, unredeemed by the passage of years. As such, these 'dead memories' can only be testified to by failed or shattered narrators – what Langer calls 'split selves', speaking orally in the present of a past from which they are forever sundered. Alas, the tragedy for several of Lanzmann's witnesses, whom he persuaded to deliver their broken testimonies to camera, was that the very exercise of revisiting this 'dead past' brought such distress to their present lives that they committed suicide.

None of the actors in *Schindler's List* suffered such a fate. Indeed, one of the survivors confessed to me after I delivered a lecture on this subject at McGill University in 1998 that it was the very 'fictionality' of *Schindler's List* which had enabled her personally to revisit her past – a revisiting which no *direct first-hand* attempt at remembrance would have permitted, leaving her psychically intact. Similar remarks have been made about such cinematic representations of the

Holocaust as *Jacob's Liar* or *Life is Beautiful*, films which are clearly closer to the fictionalist approach of *Schindler's List* than the anti-fictionalist one of Lanzmann or of Alain Resnais in *Nuit et brouillard*. The Jewish writer Aharon Appelfeld is certainly unambiguous in his claim that he could never have articulated his own death-camp nightmares except through fictional doppelgangers.

TWO: SCHINDLER'S STORY

If it is true that Spielberg deployed fictional devices, it would be wrong to accuse him of inattention to historical reality. In addition to ensuring that veracity is adhered to in every possible detail – down to the names of the shop fronts in Warsaw, where Schindler lived – Spielberg goes to great lengths to base each of the dramatised survivors of Schindler's 'list' on a real-life person. To reinforce this sense of historical verisimilitude, Spielberg chose to shoot most of the film in black and white (resisting the sensationalist lure of Technicolor). And he departs from this practice only in a few rare scenes of religious epiphany, for example the holy lighting of memorial (*Yahrzeit*) candles; the moment of Schindler's conversion, when he spots a Jewish child in a red dress marching in a line of deportees; and, most significantly, the final sequence showing the film's 'actors' walking through the cemetery in Jerusalem, accompanied by a number of still-living Schindler survivors, and placing stones of remembrance on the graves of those already departed. The fact that this closing scene is shot in colour is, paradoxically, a way of reminding us that the film is only that – a film made up of dramatised personae who cannot pretend to replace the original personages or their experiences. Spielberg's decision to subvert the aesthetic conventions of the feature film by interpolating this 'real-life' reminder thus, one could argue, prohibits conventional cinematic closure. It serves as a sort of Brechtian 'estrangement' effect to deliver us from the lure of fiction. It shows that the story goes on as history. Or, as Primo Levi counsels, that we must remember again lest it happen again.

Moreover, the charge that Spielberg is disrespectful to the singularity of Jewish suffering by casting a blond Aryan hero as saviour of the hapless Jews might actually be reversed. It could be argued that the choice of a non-Jew to play this highly dramatic role is actually a mark of respect for the uniqueness of Jewish experience (which resists such liberal dramatisation). It could be said that inviting millions of viewers across the world to see the horror of the Holocaust through the eyes of a relative outsider makes those viewers more likely to be moved – as outsiders to the event – from indifference to concern, from amnesia to awareness. And by telling the story of a non-Jew who broke with the indifference and cruelty of his own community to help Jews, he reminds Jews that there is hope that at least some outside their own community are capable of acting on their behalf.

Spielberg endeavours to recall the unimaginable trauma of the victims through images which remind us that 'this is only a film' but also that, precisely *as film*, it may bear witness to the reality of Auschwitz more graphically than any other medium. It thereby might be said to refuse what Levi has called 'the ever-repeated scene of the unlistened-to story'. By extending the solicitation to hear and listen to all potential film-goers, Schindler's List seeks to translate the memory of the event into the most accessible idiom possible without betraying the event itself. No easy task.

Aspirations did not stop there. He also went beyond the

feature-film genre to documentary. When it came to letting Jews speak of their own memories, it is significant that Spielberg did *not* choose the movie genre but opted for straightforward documentary and archival recordings. These include both the thousands of taped interviews in the Shoah History Foundation and *The Last Days* (1998), a film presented by Spielberg and directed by James Moll, which allows five Hungarian survivors of the Holocaust to return to their hometowns and deliver their own first-person testimonies. By mixing eyewitness accounts and historic footage in this way, inviting contemporary witnesses to retell the untellable journey they made from their Hungarian villages to the concentration camps and beyond, Spielberg shows that he is well aware that too much fiction can make a fool of history. He is not as diametrically opposed to the Lanzmann position as might first appear. It is perhaps best, however, to see *The Last Days* and the continuing documentary recording in the Shoah Foundation as supplements to *Schindler's List* rather than as alternatives. In the final analysis, *both* narrative modes are necessary.

THREE: SREBNIK'S STORY

In the debates about how best to represent the Holocaust, the Lanzmann line has found many advocates, notably in the artistic and academic avant-garde. In a most illuminating study, 'The Return of the Voice', Shoshana Felman argues that *Shoah* is a film where the role of the narrator is subordinated to that of interviewer and inquirer – that is, a voice which *asks* rather than tells. 'As narrator, Lanzmann does not speak', she notes, 'but rather vocally recites the words of others, lends his voice to read aloud two written documents whose authors cannot speak in their own voice.' So doing, he allows the narrative to be carried on by others – 'by the live voices of the various witnesses he interviews, whose stories must be able to speak for themselves, if they are to testify, that is, perform their unique and irreplaceable first-hand witness.' It is only by virtue of this abstention of the narrator, says Felman, that *Shoah* can in fact be an authentic narrative of testimony: 'a narrative of that precisely which can neither be reported, nor narrated, by another'. The film is thus deemed to be essentially a 'narrative of silence, the story of the filmmaker's *listening*: the narrator is the teller of the film only in so far as he is the bearer of the film's silence'.[11]

Hence the essential challenge of the film – to respect the inaccessibility of the event without colluding with it, to commemorate the victims while refusing to canonise their death as some sacred sacrifice (implied by the term 'Holocaust', which became current in the 1950s). The task is, as Felman puts it, 'to rewrite the event-without-a-witness into witnessing, and into history'.[12] *Shoah* is a film which performs the double task of breaking silence while showing the impossibility of any adequate discourse. It testifies to the unspeakability of the event while insisting on the 'absolute necessity of speaking'.[13] Indeed, Lanzmann explicitly states that his film, which took eleven years to make, is an attempt to bear witness – cinematically, through others' voices – to the impossibility of writing. (Lanzmann had originally intended to write a book about the Shoah when he went to Israel for four months.)

Lanzmann's commitment to a difficult dialectic of cinematic recreation and historical reportage is best captured, I believe, in a scene where a one-time boy singer, Simon Srebnik, returns to the concentration camp in Chelmno and relives the unbelievable moments when he was almost executed and left for dead forty years previously. This quasi-posthumous return of the survivor to the scene of the crime succeeds in conveying something of the reality of the past and the irreplaceability of the voice. Srebnik makes the journey back in time and space to the primal scene of Chelmno and delivers the following 'impossible' anachronic testimony:

> It's hard to recognise, but it was here. They burned people here. . . . Yes, this is the place. No one ever left here again. It was terrible. No one can describe it. . . . And no one can understand it. Even I, here, now. . . . I can't believe I'm here. No, I just can't believe it. It was always this peaceful here. Always. When they burned two thousand people – Jews – every day, it was just as peaceful. No one shouted. Everyone went about his work. It was silent. Peaceful. Just as it is now.

But Srebnik left there. And Srebnik describes it. He makes the impossible possible. Of the thousands of Jews sent to Chelmno two survived to tell the tale. And one of them was Srebnik. It is an incredible tale about an incredible horror. But Srebnik asks us to credit it. What happened was unbelievable, he says, but believe me, it happened![14] So doing, Srebnik defies, in my view, the apocalyptic verdict of Lyotard that the 'Shoah devours images and words – it is the death of language.' Srebnik refuses the seduction of the sublime. In spite of all, he speaks, he remembers, he tells his story.

But Lanzmann goes further still. He bears witness to the Shoah not just by enacting 'true' narrative but by exposing 'false' ones. Inviting us to see through the mendacious testimonies of certain Nazi officers and Polish villagers – and in particular a local official called Kantorowski – he re-enacts for contemporary viewers Hitler's original attempt to cover up and distort history. Thus Lanzmann manages to evoke what cannot be stated or, to use Wittgenstein's language, to *show* what cannot be *said*. The recording of Srebnik's testimony *in situ*, surrounded by one-time Polish persecutors and long-time deniers, marks the return of the repressed referent – a historical moment endured but not comprehended. It echoes the terrible truth of Valéry's line that 'our memory repeats to us what we haven't understood'.

The task of all representations of the Shoah is, it would seem, to sustain a delicate balance between (1) a historical fidelity to truth (respecting the distance of the past as it was in the past) and (2) an aesthetic fidelity to imaginative vivacity and credibility (presenting the past as if it were present). This implies a double or 'split' narrative reference to the past 'as it was' and 'as it was not'. Some contemporary narrators seek to achieve something like this by avoiding strict documentary realism in favour of a certain indirectness or inarticulateness in the witnesses' remembering – for example, David Grossman's Mamek is a eccentric child, Srebnik is a disarmed stranger, Schindler is an equivocal Aryan, etc.

In sum, if the testimony of the horror is too immediate, we are blinded by the experience. But if it is too distant, we are untouched by it. *Shoah* and *Schlindler's List* seek, in their different ways, to strike some medial point between these extremes of immediacy and remoteness.

Five

It is clear that the history of victims calls for a mode of remembering other than the ritualistic commemoration of heroes and gods. There is a crucial difference between the 'little narratives' of the vanquished and the 'Grand Narratives' of the victors. But moralists of narrative memory sometimes fail, it seems to me, to appreciate fully that reminiscence of suffering has just as much need to be *felt* as commemoration of glory. Historical horror requires to be served by an aesthetic (*aisthesis* – sensation) quite as powerful and moving as that of historical triumph – perhaps even *more* powerful if it is to compete for the attention of the public at large. It is not enough that a film like *Shoah* be shown in art-house cinemas or as high-brow TV specials on Arte and Channel 4 in Europe or PBS in America. The story of the Holocaust needs to be heard and seen by as many people as possible in each new generation. And this is at bottom an ethical demand. Hence the importance of the decision by national public television in the United States in March 1997 to screen a vivid reminder of the Holocaust which, it was legitimately feared, a whole new generation of young Americans ignored. The film which was chosen, and which provoked widespread debate throughout the schools and media networks of the entire continent, was *Schindler's List*. A phenomenon which should give some pause to the moralising elitism (however well intentioned) of Lyotard and some of his fellow avant-gardists.

Sometimes an ethics of memory is obliged to resort to aesthetics of storytelling. Viewers need not only to be made intellectually aware of the horrors of history; they also need to experience the horror of that suffering *as if* they were actually there. 'Fiction gives eyes to the horrified narrator', Paul Ricoeur rightly notes. 'Eyes to see and to weep. The present state of literature on the Holocaust provides ample proof of this. . . . One counts the cadavers or one tells the story of the victims.'[1] Memory can both inform and illustrate; and part of this illustration is the narrative use of images to *strike* us – in the sense of striking home the horror of evil or the charisma of good.

That is why in Greek culture, if you wished to communicate the virtue of courage you told the story of Achilles or Iphigenia; and if you wanted to express the meaning of vice you told the story of Circe or the Cyclops. Likewise in biblical culture, good and evil were taught not by abstract speculation but by recounting the lives of Joseph and his brothers, Moses and Mammon, or Jesus and his tormentors. It is no different when it comes to the Holocaust, though here the stakes are more contemporary and in many respects more difficult to express, especially when it means going beyond abstract statistics to the story of each single person. 'We must remind ourselves that the Holocaust was not six million', as Judith Miller writes; 'It was one, plus one, plus one.' And only in 'understanding that civilised people must defend the one, by one, by one . . . can the Holocaust, the incomprehensible, be given meaning'.[2] Stories bring the horror home to us. They singularise suffering against the anonymity of evil.

A key function of narrative memory is, I would therefore

argue, empathy. And empathy is not always escapism. It is, as Kant noted in his account of 'representative thinking' in the Third Critique, a way of identifying with as many fellow humans as possible – actors and sufferers alike – in order to participate in a common moral sense (*sensus communis*). In this manner, narrative imagination can assist what we might call a *quasi-universalisation* of remembrance, where our own memories – personal and communal – can be exchanged with others of very different times and places, where the familiar and the foreign can change hands. This is what Ricoeur means when he states that the 'horror attaches to events that must never be forgotten. It constitutes the ultimate ethical motivation for the history of victims. The victims of Auschwitz are, par excellence, the representatives for the history of all history's victims.'[3] Auschwitz is another name for six million characters in search of a story that will remind us of our forgetfulness. The essence of Hitler's plan, as one Holocaust survivor put it, was to ensure that no witness would survive to bear witness, that no executioner would dare confess the tale, and that even if either did so, *nobody would believe them*.[4] The best way to defy Hitlerism is to tell the story.

While Lanzmann's filming of the Srebnik story attests to the incomparable *singularity* of the Shoah, Spielberg's filming of Schindler's story stresses its more representative *universality*. The truth is no doubt to be found in some kind of mean which combines both ethical impulses in supplementary tension. That is what a practical wisdom of historical narrative requires in this age of easy amnesia – a proper tension between our fidelities to the *uniqueness* and *communicability* of memory.

That there are paradoxes attached to every attempt – fictional or documentary – to tell the story of the Holocaust is undeniable. As one Polish Jewish survivor put it in his book, *Music of Another World*:

> This cannot be described, for there are no words for it . . . how can one describe things that cannot be described, for which there are no words? But words must be found . . . and so every author uses words that 'did not exist' but that were within his scale of possibilities and within his knowledge of the facts. Thus contradictions were unavoidable.[5]

I think that this is a more appropriate attitude to the paradox of impossible narrative than Lawrence Langer's sometimes overly schismatic opposition between a completely collapsed version of 'chronicle', on the one hand, and a completely resolved 'historical story' on the other.[6] Curiously, this very opposition, borrowed from Hayden White, leads to the view that all narratives are consequently cut off from the 'reality' of the past and committed to some kind of consoling closure – as if every story had to end happily ever after, like the *Odyssey*, or the story of the Prodigal son or Sleeping Beauty.[7] Indeed, if one suspects that the Holocaust is an irretrievably 'dead past', it surely implies that the most authentic camp survivor would be one who resists the healing powers of narrative catharsis, who remains a stoically 'split self' condemned for ever to repeat this estranged past; or as Langer puts it, 'memory's encounter with a disintegrating time is one of the seminal themes of these testimonies'.[8]

This I find troubling. Now I fully appreciate the hard questioning by Langer, Lanzmann and Lyotard, in the face of popular fads for triumphal and heroic narrativity. And if all historical stories were indeed condemned to linear plotting, moral closure and redemptive compensation, I would consider these critics correct. But I do not believe that this is so. What I am exploring in this work is a form of narrative which can entertain its own disruption as part of its repertoire of possibilities, especially in its post-Holocaust and postmodern variations from Beckett to Primo Levi. Moreover, if what Langer calls the 'impromptu' self – expressing itself as a multiplicity of separated split selves – is all that a Holocaust survivor can truly possess, how can such a witness ever 'work through' his or her remembered past so as to become a moral agent with some kind of narrative selfhood and constancy, capable of healing, acting or forgiving?[9] My question here is, in short: can a non-self condemned to non-stories ever really escape from Auschwitz?

The need to retell is clearly, I submit, as unavoidable as the impossibility of doing so. Helen Bamber describes this paradox well in her account of counselling after her arrival in Belsen after the War:

> [I] would be sitting there in one of those chilly rooms, on a rough blanket on a bed, and the person [I] was talking to would suddenly begin to tell [me] what they had seen, or try to tell what it was like. . . . Above all else there was the need to tell you everything, over and over and over.[10]

Eventually Bamber realised that what was most important in all this was to 'listen and to receive this' as if it were part of you and that the act of taking and showing that you were available was itself playing some useful role. A sort of mourning beneath and beyond tears: 'it wasn't so much grief as a pouring out of some ghastly vomit like a kind of horror'.[11] What Bamber's accounts of these first-hand testimonies make evident, no less than those of Lawrence Langer's, is that Holocaust stories are to be understood less as heroic tales of 'triumph over adversity' than as impossible narratives that the survivors themselves insist on narrating in order to survive their survival.

One especially vivid account of a theatrical testimony in Belsen says this with excruciating poignancy. The play in Yiddish was performed for remaining survivors after the liberation by other survivors. It re-enacted a family at table and was received in total silence by the audience:

> The family portrayed would be obviously an orthodox family; and then the Nazis would come in. And they would drag or kill the mother; and the power of the scene turned around the abuse of the mother, and the break-up of the family. The depiction of the Nazis was realistic and violent. The sense of disaster about to happen could be felt in that hall. Nothing explicit about the aftermath was shown, as I remember it. I have never seen anything so effective, despite the crudity of the stage and the performance. It was raw and so close to the experience of the audience. There was never any applause. Each time it was like a purging.[12]

Aristotle would have called this purgation by pity and fear, catharsis. And I believe that *Schindler's List* and certain other dramatised representations in film or fiction may be viewed as attempts, however flawed and failed, to replicate this kind of catharsis for later generations who otherwise might never be able to imagine what the horror was like.

I have chosen the Shoah as my primary case study for historical narrative as it is an event 'at the limit' which, as such, questions the very nature, power and scope of storytelling. As

Habermas says, 'Auschwitz has changed the basis for the continuity of the conditions of life within history.'[13] But while the Shoah puts the very narratability of certain events into question, it also carries a summons to remember the truth of these events which cannot be met, I believe, without the aid of testimonial narrative. So we are left with the difficult task of trying to decide how best to narrate the history of an event which runs the risk, on being narrated, of losing its unique character of unspeakable horror. It seems to me in view of our above discussions that there are a number of pitfalls that narrative must try to avoid here:

(1) the danger of becoming some kind of Master Narrative which explains it all away – for example the Holocaust is a sacrifice willed by God (the fundamentalist argument), a necessary 'final solution' (the Nazi argument), or a logical response to the threat of Bolshevism (the German revisionist argument);

(2) the danger of disintegrating into a medley of relativistic micro-narratives: the view that the Shoah can be told in a thousand different ways – pro-Jewish, pro-Nazi, pro-communist, etc. – and you can take your pick since any one of these language games is as good as the next (for example Syberberg's Hitler: Ein Film aus Deutschland);

(3) the danger of banalising the Holocaust by reducing it to voyeuristic spectacle or kitsch (D. M. Thomas's White Hotel, Caviani's Night Porter, the TV Holocaust series and certain sensationalist memorials);

(4) the opposite danger of reducing this event to a cult of the sublime: an object so exceptional and incomparable as to escape all historical representation; or so monstrous that it can only, at most, be obliquely evoked by rare aesthetic

experiments (for example the late poetry of Paul Celan or elite avant-garde exhibitions);

(5) the related danger of certain postmodern arguments that the narratives of the Shoah, like all other narratives, are bound to the self-referentiality of language and so can make no truth-claim to any kind of reality outside of the narrative texts themselves (what Baudrillard calls 'irreference');

(6) the danger of testimonial narrative being dismissed altogether in the name of some putative 'scientific' account of the 'objective facts' (for example certain negationist and positivist historians);

(7) the danger of narrative being repudiated in the name of total silence (as in Adorno's maxim 'After Auschwitz who can write poetry?', or Lyotard's analogy with an earthquake so horrendous as to destroy all recording instruments).[14]

And so we are faced, in sum, with a double duty – to narrate the event and yet to respect its inevitable difference from other events. The Shoah is where the politics of memory and the aesthetics of representation converge in critical fashion. It poses for us the central problem of how we move from micro-narratives of multiple singular testimony to certain quasi-universal narratives that might be shared by as many people as possible without succumbing to the illusion of some absolute scientific consensus. To help this transition we need, I believe, an ethic of free public discussion: the sort of discourse ethics advanced by Habermas and Apel, which could explore the necessary conditions for a narrative counting as historically true – for example consistency of memories, coherence of testimonies, credibility of witnesses, confirmation of referential evidence, public sharing of truth-claims, appropriateness of narrative genres, effectiveness of account, moral persuasiveness of justice-claims, etc. – while acknowledging that no one of these criteria is sufficient in itself. Without such a public conversation about the validity of our testimonies it is difficult to avoid the polar extremes of (a) dogmatic realism (it just happened that way) or (b) sceptical relativism (no one can say that it happened at all).

I conclude, therefore, that narrative remembrance can help us represent the past as it really *was* or reinvent it as it might have been. For fiction, the role of reinvention is what matters most – even in historical novels like *War and Peace*. But in cases of psychotherapeutic and historical testimony – like those of Dora and Schindler – I have been arguing that the function of veridical recall claims primacy. Distinguishing between these two separate, if often overlapping, functions is, I submit, of crucial ethical import. As is discerning *when* it is right to remember and *when* it is right to forget. Or, indeed, *how much* we should remember and forget. Sometimes, some places – Northern Ireland, Bosnia, Rwanda – it is important to let go of history, to heed Nietzsche's counsel to 'actively forget' the past in order to overcome the instincts of resentment and revenge. At such times we must resist the frenzy of fanatic commemoration, heeding Brian Friel's maxim that 'to remember everything is a form of madness'. Other times, other places – Auschwitz being the time and place par excellence – it is essential to remember the past in order to honour our 'debt to the dead' and try to insure that it never happens again.[15]

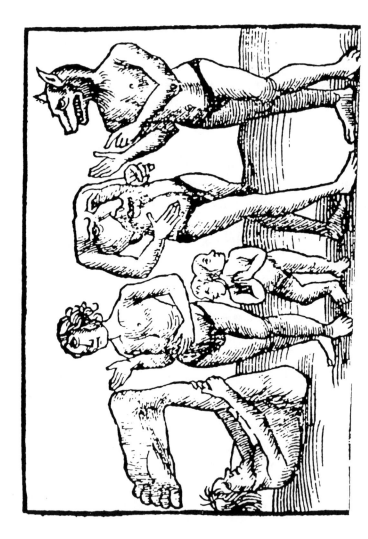

Figure 1: Strangers beyond the nation were often pictured as mutant monsters (appeared in James Axtell, *Beyond 1492*, New York, Oxford University Press, 1992)

Figure 2: Native Americans were demonised as savage animals who needed to be saved by the arriving European Pilgrims (School, Portuguese Hell, mid-sixteenth century, Museu Nacional de Arte Antiga, Lisbon. By kind permission of Giraudon/Art Resource, New York)

Figure 3: Typical caricature of the Irish as treacherous beasts, which was common fare in popular British magazines like *Punch* (John Tenniel, 'Two Forces', first published in *Punch*, 29 October 1881)

Figure 4: The Negro slave and simianised Irish immigrant were at one time equally threatening to the Puritan new world ('The Ignorant Vote: Honors are Easy', *Harper's Weekly*, December 1876)

Figure 5: Captain America warns the nation that invading aliens could be anyone anywhere (vol. 3, issue 6, June 1998, *Captain America*, TM & © 2001 Marvel Characters, Inc. Used with permission)

Figure 6: The opening scene from *Men in Black* exposes extra-terrestrial aliens disguised as illegal non-resident aliens sneaking across the Mexican–US border (*Men in Black*, Amblin Entertainment–Columbia Tristar. Reproduced by kind permission of Ronald Grant Archives)

Part Three
National Narratives: Rome, Britain, America

Introduction

Six

The exaltation of origins can take violent forms because one wants an enemy; and as the enemy is not communism any more – because it doesn't exist – the enemy will be the other . . . the other nation, the other ethnic group, the scapegoat.

Julia Kristeva[1]

Historical communities are constituted by the stories they recount to themselves and to others. Hence the importance of the rectification that contemporary historians bring to bear on the historical accounts of their predecessors. This is as true of the 'new histories' of British–Irish relations (1798, the Famine, 1916, 1969) as it is of the French and American debates on the meaning of their respective national Revolutions. But questions of historical revision and reinvention go back to the beginnings of Western civilisation, and are to be found in the genesis stories of its two major foundation cultures: Graeco-Roman and biblical. Both provide us with classic instances of *nations as narrations*.

While the Greeks and Romans relied largely on the mythologies of gods and heroes recounted by poets like Hesiod, Homer and Virgil, biblical Israel relied on the 'revealed' narratives of Genesis, Exodus and Kings, which succeeding generations recounted and reinterpreted (making Judaism the 'culture of the Book' par excellence). Moreover, biblical stories add a future-oriented or eschatological dimension to the recall of ancient events. Thomas Mann describes this sense of narrative historicity well in *Joseph and his Brothers* when he has Jacob initiate the young Tamar into the rites of Hebrew storytelling:

> The 'once upon a time' was still fresh, and Jacob's voice shook . . . for these were all God-stories, sacred in the telling. But it is quite certain now that Tamar's listening soul in the course of instruction was fed not alone on historical, time-overlaid once-upon-a-time, the time-honoured 'once', but with 'one day' as well. And 'one day' is a word of scope, it has two faces. It looks back, into solemnly twilit distances, and it looks forwards, far, far forwards, into space, and is not less solemn because it deals with the to-be than that other dealing with the has-been. . . . Into all [Jacob's] stories of the beginning there came an element of promise, so that one could not tell them without foretelling.[2]

Christianity redeployed this same narrative tradition, the Gospels comprising four testimonies by four different evangelists. One of these evangelists, Luke, leaves us in little doubt about the central role of narrativity in the transmission of Messianic memory:

> Since many have undertaken to compile a narrative of the events that have been fulfilled among us, just as those who were eyewitnesses from the beginning and ministers of the word have handed them down to us, I too have decided, after investigating everything accurately anew, to write it down in an orderly sequence.
>
> (Luke 1: 1–4)

Moreover, it is precisely because stories proceed from stories in such a manner that historical communities are ultimately responsible for the formation and re-formation of their own identity. One cannot remain constant over the passage of historical time – and therefore remain faithful to one's promises and covenants – unless one has some minimal remembrance of where one comes from, and of how one came to be what one is. In this sense, identity is memory. As Hegel put it, *das Wesen ist das Gewesene*. 'What is is what it has become.' Or more simply, the past is always present.

But along with every culture's sense of *constancy* over time goes an attendant imperative of *innovation*. The 'one day' of narrativity bears a double visage, to use Mann's metaphor. For once one recognises that one's identity is fundamentally narrative in character, one discovers an ineradicable openness and indeterminacy at the root of collective memory. Each nation discovers that it is at heart an 'imagined community' (in Benedict Anderson's phrase), that is, a narrative construction to be reinvented and reconstructed again and again. The benefit of such discovery is that it becomes more difficult to make the mistake of taking oneself *literally*, of assuming that one's inherited identity *goes without saying*. And that is why I would argue that the tendency of a nation towards xenophobia or insularity can be resisted by its own narrative resources to imagine itself otherwise – through its own eyes or those of others.

The problem is not that each society constructs itself as a story but that it forgets that it has done so. Whenever a nation forgets its own narrative origins it becomes dangerous. Self-oblivion is the disease of a community that takes itself for granted – or like an overgrown narcissistic infant presumes that it is the centre of the world, entitled to assert itself to the detriment of others. When this happens the nation congeals into a terrifying will-to-power. The result is totalitarianism, fascism and fanaticism. These political pathologies are symptoms of the same erasure: the denial of the birth of every nation in narration of some kind. Whence Adorno's adage, 'all reification is forgetting'. That is why the solution to many national conflicts may well reside in the willingness of both disputants – for example Arab and Israeli, Nationalist and Unionist, Serb and Croat, Tutsi and Hutu – to *exchange narrative memories*. For such mutual translation of competing stories might eventually enable the adversaries to see each other through alternative eyes.

If warring nations were able to acknowledge their own and the other's narrative identities they might then be able to reimagine themselves in new ways. Blocked and fixated memories, trapped in compulsive repetition and resentment, could then find the freedom to remember the past differently, historical enemies recognising themselves as mirror-images. It is only by means of such emancipatory remembering, I would suggest, that genuine acts of pardon may release reified pasts into futures. Effective amnesty issues not from amnesia but from the acknowledgement of different ways of signifying a debt to the dead which invites us to recreate ourselves in the light of novel options. It is not the proper role of any peace and justice tribunal, for example, to efface the memory of crimes but to retell these crimes in such a way that we may be freer, if we choose, to dissolve the debt they have accrued. 'Forgiveness is a sort of healing of memory, the completion of its mourning period. Delivered from the weight of debt, memory is liberated for great projects. Forgiveness gives memory a future.'[3] It would not be a contradiction to say, therefore, that amnesty is the corollary of 'critical memory' even as it is the contrary of 'repetition memory'.

Caution is clearly called for here. Candide has no role in

this play of critical remembering. Only those who have done the narrative 'working through' of the past are really in a position to let go of it – to forgive and forget justly. Narrative memory cannot afford to be naive, for stories are never innocent. Each retelling of history is part of a continuing conflict of interpretations. A battlefield of competing meanings. Why? Because every history is told from a certain perspective and in the light of specific prejudices (in Gadamer's sense). Narrative remembrance, I repeat, is not always on the side of the angels. It can as easily lead to false consciousness and ideological dissimulation as to openness and tolerance. This distorting power is, admittedly, underestimated by most contemporary advocates of narrative ethics – MacIntyre, Nussbaum, Booth – who tend to downplay the need for a hermeneutics of critical suspicion. But it is equally neglected by certain postmodern disciples of Nietzsche's *Second Untimely Considerations*, who believe that it is sufficient to 'actively forget the past' to have done with it. Those who think that they can dispense with historical narrative by fiat may ultimately be dispensed with by it.

Seven

The civilisation of Rome, like that of most world cultures, was founded on stories. And here again we must cast a suspecting glance towards its most influential inaugural myths, recalling Walter Benjamin's phrase that every document of civilisation is written over a tale of barbarism. Rome was founded upon the myth of a perfect marriage between the goddess of beauty and the god of triumph. The former, Venus, was the mother of Aeneas; the latter, Mars, was the father of Romulus. This sacred union of divinities was consecrated in the Roman pantheon by the Emperor Augustus, and the respective offspring, Aeneas and Romulus, became the two most revered heroes of the new Empire. But if we look at the stories of Aeneas and Romulus more closely, we begin to detect traces of originary violence beneath their official sanctity.

Aeneas's mother, Venus, arose from the blood of Cronus's castrated genitals. Aeneas's father, Anchises, whom he carried on his back out of the burning city of Troy, instilled such filial piety that Aeneas abandoned his beloved Dido, thus precipitating her violent suicide. Mixing snippets of actual history (*res gestae*) with imaginary tales and myths, Virgil founded Rome upon a good story – one that covers blood-and-betrayal subplots with a super-plot of ineluctable divinity. It may well be true that some of the early Romans who built their city on the Tiber did in fact travel from a walled city called Troy situated south of the Hellespont on the eastern Aegean coast. But if it was historically possible that Trojans like Aeneas founded Rome, they were certainly not descended from the Goddess Venus or directed to Italy by the prophecy of Neptune and the will of Apollo!

Virgil's fantastic narrative, in short, is an attempt to combine story and history so as to suggest that Rome owes its origins to both a celestial order of divine blessing and a temporal order of genealogical events. And the basic persuasion that this 'mixed' narrative of fantasy and fact promotes is that the great Roman Empire of Augustus was historically and theologically *inevitable*.

Hayden White identifies the rationale behind the commingling of history and fiction well when he describes 'story' as a process of 'selection and arrangement of data from the *unprocessed historical record* in the interest of rendering the record more comprehensible to an *audience* of a particular kind'.[1] Where a so-called 'chronicle' was content to report a sequence of happenings as they occurred, 'story' contrives to insert a specific sense of perspective and purpose into the otherwise aimless chronology. Story introduces the concordance of plot – in other words, it strives to 'emplot' the medley of events into some beginning-middle-and-end (though not necessarily in that order). The transmutation of chronicle into story occurs when some events are characterised as inaugural, others as transitional and others again as terminal. The plot turns the 'and then and then and then' of mere sequential events into a recounting according to some *design*, however fantastical it may be. And for some reason, people from the beginning of time have felt a need for such plot and purpose. The Romans were no exception.

The genesis of Romulus is even more ambivalent. While ostensibly relating the story of two brothers surviving miraculously in the wilds, thanks to the protection of gods and a she-wolf, before growing up to become the founders of Rome, the narrative carries a more sombre lining. Romulus and his brother were the result of the rape of their mother, Rhea Silvia, by Mars – a violent origin replicated in Romulus's eventual murder of his own twin, Remus. Behind the *mythos* of glory runs a sub-*mythos* of brutality and blood. As if the foundation myth is telling a double tale of elevated and abyssal origins.

Both foundation myths, according to Pascale Guignard and other commentators, are predicated upon the expulsion of the Etruscan 'other' whom the Romans displaced and ultimately destroyed. The foundation stories thus served as a kind of cover-up, masking memories of primordial blood-letting beneath the official mythology of divine genealogy (Mars and Venus) and heroic ancestry (Aeneas and Romulus).

So doing, the Romans were reiterating the ancient Greek practice of dividing the world into 'humans' and 'barbarians'. And this very binary division into pure and impure is in all cases dialectically tied to a repressed 'primal scene' of violent expulsion and purgation. Moreover, the carry-over of primitive Bacchic rites from Greece into Rome itself signals the co-existence, at least at the level of the symbolic unconscious, of surface civility with subterranean traces of originary blood-letting. As the *Bacchae* of Euripides had already suggested, the city is founded on the sacrificial killing of a scapegoat who draws all the internal violence from the community onto itself and thus procures an inaugural moment of peace. This is what ultimately guarantees the sacrificial victim's subsequent divination by the redeemed community. The victim is retrospectively commemorated as the one who first saved them from themselves!

Euripides's dramatic narrative relates the violent killings of Dionysus by the Maenads and of King Pentheus by his own mother, who tears him apart with her bare hands and eats his body raw. The ritual retelling of Dionysiac sacrifice was associated in turn with orgiastic inebriation and the wearing of animal masks – other mnemonic remnants of those archaic 'others', the Etruscans, who were vanquished by Rome but never vanished from its unconscious. One particular anecdote is telling. In 401, when Rome was invaded by foreigners, a pair of wolves attacked the Emperor, and in their lupine entrails were found two human hands. This was read as a return of the 'other'. The Etruscan wolves that nourished Romulus and Remus were revisiting the Empire that had renounced them.[2]

The original purpose of mythologies, for Rome as for all major empires and nations, was to provide its people with a sense of 'original identity'. Ritualistic recounting of myths of origin were thought to repair the fractures of the present by invoking some primordial event which occurred at the birth of time – in illo tempore – and so revive a feeling of primordial oneness and belonging. Such narratives of genesis were often linked to tales of fatherland and motherland, serving as potent symbols for reanimating the power of 'dead generations' and establishing a conviction of unruptured continuity with one's tradition. If this conviction was successfully sustained, the narratives came to serve as national myths of sovereignty.

Myths were thus deemed to convey some kind of prim-ordial power to the extent that they narrated a sacred history, namely, a trans-human and trans-temporal epiphany which allegedly took place in the Holy Time of the Great Beginning. Mythic narratives tended to become exemplary and repeatable, operating as a paradigm which explained and legitimised human actions in the present. 'By *imitating* the exemplary acts of mythic deities and heroes', writes Mircea Eliade, 'man detaches himself from profane time and magically re-enters the Great Time, the Sacred Time.'[3] Myths made sure that the past was never totally past.

This synchronising power of mythic narrative is often contrasted with the 'hot' historicity of Enlightenment progress.[4] But things are not so simple. In the national narratives of many modern nations, for example, both forms of temporality – hot and cold, progressivist and mythic – overlap to form a strangely ambivalent experience: a sort of double time referring to *both* the atemporal origin *and* the here and now.[5] This is what happened in the French Revolution when Robespierre and the Jacobins celebrated the progression of enlightened history, marching from the present into the future, while simultaneously harking back to the mythic timelessness of Rome in its first beginnings. Several of the French revolutionaries even wore Roman togas and other classical garb to the great Convention meetings in Paris in the 1790s.

The foundational narratives of Rome epitomise the essential meaning of tradition – from the Latin *tradere*, to transfer – carrying as it does the present into the past and the past into the present. Like Aeneas ferrying his father Anchises on his back. Hence we find that the mythic narratives of tradition often defy the normal logic of *either/or* by combining such opposed orders as sacred and profane, peace and violence, divine and human, redeemed and damned. *Mythos* confronts us with a specific logic of imagination where the laws of

contradiction and causality no longer apply. 'The alternative
either–or cannot be expressed in the process of dreaming', as
Freud noted. 'Both of the alternatives are usually inserted in
the text of the dream as though they were equally valid.'[6]
Many contemporary commentators of myth – from Lévi-
Strauss and Eliade to Hillman and Campbell – agree on the
fact that originary modes of storytelling, impelled by the need
to conflate and conquer contradictions, never fully disappear
from the world of the psyche; they merely alter and mask
their operations.

But mythos is by no means all sweetness and light. If not
acknowledged as a central part of our unconscious psyche,
or given adequate expression in our dreams, art-works or
religions, mythic stories can assume sinister proportions.
Whence the rise of ideological cults of fascist and totali-
tarian leaders or sacrificial myths of scapegoating and
anti-Semitism, a phenomenon trenchantly exposed by
'demythologising' critics like Girard and Bultmann.

It is probably fair to say, on the basis of our cursory review
of the classic foundation stories of Greece and Rome, that
myths are neither good nor bad but interpretation makes them
so. It is not usually stories in themselves that transfigure or dis-
figure, but the uses and practices to which we put them and
the interests and aims we have them serve. Mythos is a two-way
street. It can lead to perversion (bigotry, racism, fascism) or
to liberation (the reactivation of a genuine social imaginary
open to universal horizons). If we need to de-mythologise,
we also need to re-mythologise. And this double process
requires a discrimination between authentic and inauthentic
uses of mythic storytelling. For if originary stories are sometimes a response to repression, they can bring new repression
in their own right. This is why it is necessary to see how

founding narratives can emancipate or incarcerate, how they can generate symbols of empowerment or idols of bewitchment.

At best, the originary stories of Greece, Rome and other formative cultures invite us to reimagine our past in ways which challenge the status quo and open up alternative modes of thinking. At worst, they engender revivalist shibboleths of fixed identity, closing off dialogue with all that is other than themselves. Without the great foundational narratives – classical or biblical – we in the West risk capitulating to the blind conformism of fact. Granted. But if idolised as ideological doctrines, and sundered from the real, these same narratives can mutate into another kind of conformity. That is why we need to keep our mythological memories in critical dialogue with history. And, by extension, why every culture must go on telling stories, inventing and reinventing its inherited imaginary, lest its history congeal into dogma.

Eight

Foundational narratives were by no means confined to the Greeks and Romans. And in the remainder of Part 3, I propose to look at the emergence of two different dialectics of national narrative in modern Western history. Given my own experience as a native of the islands of Ireland and Britain, currently teaching and residing in America, I shall take my next examples from those stories I know best. I begin with the British–Irish case before moving on to its American counterpart.

Like most narratives of national genesis, the modern story of British and Irish identity began with a mirror-stage. The British and Irish peoples first identified themselves as unique by differentiating themselves from one another. A formative chapter in this process, noted by Welsh historian R. R. Davies, was the attempt to forge the notion of a proto-British English nation (*natio* or *gens*) over and against that of a colonised Irish nation in the fourteenth century. The English settlers of the time felt so fearful of mingling with the natives – thereby becoming 'more Irish than the Irish themselves' – that they invented the infamous Statutes of Kilkenny (ratified in 1366). These Statutes instigated segregation between coloniser and colonised, fomenting political divisions between two supposedly incompatible 'peoples'. Non-observance of the Statutes was called 'degeneracy' – that is, betrayal of the *gens*.

To marry outside the *gens* was to cease to be a proper English 'gentlemen', thereby forfeiting the attendant virtues of gentility and gentrification. Commingling with the so-called Gaelic natives was, as the old phrase went, 'going beyond the Pale' (literally, exiting from the frontier-walls of the city of settlers, Dublin). To transgress this boundary limit was to betray the tribe.

The colonising *gens* came to define itself, accordingly, over and against its *de-gens*, its alter ego: namely, the native Irish. Thus, even though it was the Venerable Bede who initially invoked the idea of an English *gens*, with Alfred's expansion of Wessex (871–99) paving the way, it was arguably in the laboratory of Ireland that the English nation first saw itself in the glass – and believed its own image. In Ireland, the English learned to fashion their official story, to forge their history by way of securing their credentials as a *separate nation*. If the Irish didn't exist, the English would have had to invent them.

By virtue of this mimetic narration, the Irish in turn began redefining themselves as an equally pure and distinct *natio*. And here again the politics of identity was ultimately founded upon a narrative of separatism. In response to the colonial campaign of segregation, King Donald O'Neill of Ulster wrote to the Pope in 1317 declaring himself heir of the 'whole of Ireland' and narrating an unbroken historical continuity of the Irish people (*gens*) through their laws, speech and long memory of tribulations suffered at the hands of the colonial invaders. The Irish, in short, wrote themselves back into history in response to the English attempt to write them out of it. Irish apologetics echoed, as defence strategy, English apartheid.

What both narrations masked, however, was that the colonial settlers, no less than the Irish natives, were descended from the same mongrelised mix of successive ethnic invasions and migrations – Viking, Anglo-Norman, Scots, Celtic, Milesian, etc. As recent research has shown, the peoples of both islands share virtually the same gene pool. But even regardless of genetic considerations, I think it is true to say that since the act of reciprocal narration in the fourteenth century, the Irish and the English have evolved like twins, inseparable in their loves and hates, joined at the hip of Ulster and for ever bound to a common story of conflict and reconciliation. As Douglas Hyde, the first President of the Irish State, wittily remarked: 'The English are the people we love to hate and never cease to imitate.'[1]

In sum, the first successful attempt to tell the story of the Irish and the British as two separate peoples really took hold only after the fourteenth-century invasionary settlement made it in the interests of the colonisers and the colonised to differentiate themselves as two distinct *gentes*. The criteria of differentiation were conventional rather than natural. They were, in other words, less ethnic than cultural and legal in character, having to do with apparel, residency, name-forms, language, property rights, traditions and memories. The *gens* actually 'looked' almost identical to the *de-gens*, and they often shared the same surnames. But this very absence of distinguishing racial marks made it all the *more* necessary to compensate at the level of contrived legislation and statute. Where nature could not segregate, law would try to do so.

But law was not enough. The border of the Pale separating *gens* from *de-gens* remained largely porous and indeterminable, requiring repeated recourse to propaganda narratives. And so Official Stories of 'them' and 'us' began to take hold. The stereotyping usually assumed the guise of prejudice and snobbery ('the natives are not *gentlemen*' . . .), drawing great ammunition from Giraldus Cambrensis's twelfth-century *History and Topography of Ireland*. Cambrensis himself was a better storyteller than he was a chronicler. That is to say, his accounts were not so much accurate empirical observations as propagandistic fantasies. Cambrensis was, tellingly, a secretary to Prince John on one of his invasive expeditions to Ireland, and his colourful narrative of the natives as 'a wild and inhospitable people who live like beasts' well served its colonial purposes. As the Irish historian Art Cosgrove would later observe, 'The picture drawn by Gerald was unflattering; the Irish were economically backward, politically fragmented, wild, untrustworthy and semi-pagan, and guilty of sexual immorality. Doubtless the picture was much influenced by the need to justify conquest and dispossession.' But the prize for colonial stereotypes must surely go to the British historian Charles Kingsley, who, many centuries after Gerald, could still remark on a visit to Ireland: 'to see white chimpanzees is dreadful; if they were black, one would not feel it so much, but their skins are as white as ours!'. This caricature of the Irish as 'the white Negro' was to prove pervasive as a legitimising force of colonial superiority, as the graphic portraits in Perry Curtis's *Apes and Angels* illustrate.[2]

So if we could say that *Beowulf*'s Grendel and her kind served as a mythological 'other' in the formation of Anglo-Saxon identity – the monster is referred to in the Old English saga as an 'alien fiend' (*ellor-gast*) – the simianised Irish Caliban came to play the role of its historical descendant. The scapegoated stranger haunting the unstable borders of both nation and psyche became a recurring ingredient of the Anglo-Saxon story – that 'fiend out of hell' (to follow Heaney's translation of *Beowulf*) who stalked the 'marshes and desolate fens . . .

dwelling among banished monsters, Cain's clan whom the Creator had outlawed and condemned as outcasts'.[3] In the shifting frontier zones of Irish–English relations – no less than in those of Dane, Swede and Geat recorded in *Beowulf* – the inaugural scene of 'pure people' versus 'impure monster' raised its hoary head again and again. What we might call a Mythological Return of the Same.

The Irish, of course, responded with their own narratives of self-conscious national pride. From the early middle ages on, we witness many local poets and bards spinning powerful tales of the virginal motherland being raped and plundered by the invading *Sasanach*. And this widening gender opposition between Ireland as feminine victim-virgin (Roisín Dubh, Caitlín ní Houlihán, *Spéirbhean*) and England as masculine master (fatherland, King and country, etc.) was accentuated by the emergence of a powerful national literature which underscored the separateness of both peoples.[4]

But while literary stories worked, they were as nothing compared to the divisionary power of religious stories. Arguably, it wasn't really until the seventeenth-century plantation of Ulster, after the Reformation, that the colonisation of Ireland ultimately *succeeded* – and with a vengeance. With the disenfranchising of Irish Catholics *en masse* in favour of planter Protestants, religious narratives of biblical election, divine right and Puritan evangelism were frequently deployed as radical forces of segregation. While neither nature nor law nor literature was able to divide the peoples of the two islands, the flaming sword of biblical narrative would.

After Elizabethan and Cromwellian fantasies of Protestant purity had done their work, there were many Protestants and Catholics in the island of Ireland who preferred to die rather than commingle. So that even Wolfe Tone and the United

Irishmen, with their valiant story of a single nation of 'Catholic, Protestant and Dissenter' in the 1790s, could not put the Hibernian Humpty Dumpty back together again. Sectarianism was there to stay.

It would take another two hundred years after the failed Rebellion of 1798 for Britain and Ireland mutually to renounce their separatist stories (of suprematism and martyrdom respectively), thereby permitting Irish Catholics, Protestants and Dissenters to co-habit peaceably for the first time since the Reformation. Only when the Irish and British communities inhabiting Ulster learned to *retell* their stories (greatly helped by their writers and historians), and to acknowledge that they could be 'British or Irish or both', could they be reconciled. Not as a unitary national identity, of course, but as a multiple post-national one where a thousand stories could be told. British and Irish, Unionist and Nationalist, Loyalist and Republican, eventually came to realise that there were no essential identities carved from opposing cliffs, only 'imagined communities' that could be reimagined in alternative ways. The different nations discovered slowly and painfully that they were, at bottom, constituted by different narrations. And this discovery set them free.

Just as concealing narratives had maimed, revealing narratives promised to heal. The hair of the dog that bit. Good stories undoing bad ones. For the time being, at least.

The stories of the genesis of English and Irish nationalities might thus be said, despite the asymmetry of colonisers and colonised, to run broadly in parallel. Because the English, in sum, had difficulty accepting that the islands of Britain and Ireland were made up of 'multiple' peoples due to waves of successive migrations – culminating in the Viking and

Norman invasions – they struggled to invent a sense of pure, uncontaminated identity by demonising the Irish as 'other'. Thus while the peoples of England (including the Normans) were by the fifteenth century welded into an integrative unit by virtue of strategies of alien-nation – namely, by establishing one nation over against another – the island of Ireland remained a symptom of such divisions. But the contrived national unity of Englishness, and of Britishness after the union with Wales and Scotland, would forever be haunted by the ghost of its alien and alienated double: Ireland. The very *difference* from Irishness became intrinsic to the British Empire's narrative identity. Its Hibernian 'other' was uncannily mirrored in its own self-image, the familiar spectre hidden in strangeness, the original double the British had forgotten to remember, the menacing *revenant* of their own political unconscious.[5]

Linda Colley provides further and more specific evidence for this mirror-imaging of Irish and British nationalism in the last two centuries. In *Britons: Forging the Nation, 1797–1837*, she elaborates the basic point that the peoples that made up Britain were brought together as a national narrative by confrontation with the 'other'.[6] In keeping with the theses of the new British history advocated by Benedict Anderson, Hugh Kearney, J. G. A. Pocock and Tom Nairn, Colley suggests that British national identity is contingent and relational (like most others) and is best understood as an *interaction* between several different histories and stories. It is Colley's thesis that most inhabitants of the 'British Isles' laid claim to a double, triple or multiple identity – even after the consolidation of British national identity around 1700. So that it would not be unusual, for example, to find someone identifying him- or herself as a citizen of Edinburgh, a Lowlander, a Scot and a

Briton. It was over and against this pluralist practice of identification, on the ground, that the artificial nation of Great Britain managed to forge itself, not only by its Tudor consolidation and successive annexations of Wales in 1536, Scotland in 1707 and Ireland in 1800, but by a series of external wars between 1689 and 1815 and also, of course, by its massive Industrial Revolution and overseas trade expansion. In this manner, Britain managed to extend its empire over half the globe and to unify its citizens back home by replicating on a world stage what England had first tried out in Ireland in the fourteenth century. It galvanised its peoples into national unity by pitting them against external enemies.

The strategic benefits of British imperialism were not just commercial and political, therefore, but psychic as well. And the biggest advantage of the 'overseas' African and Asian colonies was that, unlike Britain's traditional enemies closer to home (the Irish and the French), these 'others' actually *looked* entirely different. But as the Empire began to fracture in the first part of the twentieth century, the British resorted to *religion* once again to confirm the narrative of national identity. What united the British above all else in times of trouble was their story of 'common Protestantism' (ensuring to this day that the Sovereign of the United Kingdom is a member of the established Anglican Church). Hence the emblematic importance of the famous image of St Paul's in London during the Blitz, the cathedral of the besieged Empire par excellence 'emerging defiantly and unscathed from the fire and devastation surrounding it . . . a Protestant citadel, encircled by enemies, but safe under the watchful eye of a strictly English-speaking deity'.[7]

The British nation thus emerged, like many another nation, as a *narrated community* which invented itself in dialectical opposition to its 'others' – and most especially to Ireland, its first, last and most intimate rival, combining as it did three of the most significant characteristics of alien-nation: (1) Ireland was predominantly *Catholic* (non-Protestant); (2) it was a *colony* (overseas if only a little over – but sufficiently to be treated like a subordinate rather than an equal neighbour like Wales or Scotland); and (3) Ireland was a traditional ally of *France*, the main military rival to British imperial designs, and inspirational insurrectionary model, along with Ireland, for rebellious movements in India, Palestine and elsewhere. Thus Ireland came to serve as the untrustworthy 'poor relation' in the drama of the Empire's rise and fall.

It is, of course, the very 'ambiguity' of Ireland's insider–outsider relation with Britain that made it at once so fascinating for the British *and* so repellent. The fascination was witnessed in London's passion for Irish writing and drama from Swift and Sheridan to Wilde, Yeats and Shaw; while the repulsion found expression in countless Fleet Street stories of the Irish as brainless simian brutes. This paradox of attraction and recoil is typical of what Edward Said calls 'orientalism': Ireland serving as Britain's Orient in its own backyard. It also approximates to what Freud describes as the 'uncanny' (*Das Unheimliche*) – the return of the familiar as unfamiliar, of friend as foe. Ireland served, one might say, as Britain's unconscious reminding it that it was ultimately and irrevocably a stranger to itself: that its self-identity was in fact constructed upon the screening of its forgotten 'other' – in both senses of 'screen': to conceal and to project.

The nature of this unsettling dialectic was evident not only in the mirror-plays of Irish dramatists like Shaw and Wilde, but also in the works of English dramatists who reflected on their neighbouring island. Already in Shakespeare we find soundings. In *Henry V*, for example, we encounter Captain MacMorris, the first true-blue Irishman to appear in English letters, posing the conundrum: 'What *ish* my nation?' So doing, MacMorris recalls not only that Ireland is a nation still in question (i.e. in quest of itself), but that England is too. And we find an even more explicit example in *Richard II*, when the King visits Ireland only to regain the British mainland disoriented and dismayed. Having set out secure in his sovereignty, he returns wondering what exactly his identity *is* and, by implication, his legitimacy as monarch: 'I had forgot myself, am I not king?' he puzzles. 'Is not the king's name twenty thousand names?' (III, ii). In short, Ireland takes its revenge on the King by multiplying the one and indivisible nature of his sovereignty. It upsets the storyline, reverses the plot and subverts the central role of the protagonist. Astray in his Irish colony, the King finds himself upstaged and without lines. And thus deconstructed, he discovers that the very notion of a united national kingdom is nominal rather than real, existing in name rather than in fact.[8]

The British narrative of Empire has collapsed in recent times. This has been brought on by a variety of factors, including: (1) the final forfeiting of the overseas colonies (epitomised by the Hong Kong handover); (2) the end of the Protestant hegemony (with the mass immigration to the British mainland of non-Protestants from ex-colonies – including Ireland); (3) the entry of the United Kingdom, however hesitantly, into the Single European Union, which ended Britain's isolationist stance vis-à-vis its European alien-nations, Ireland, France and Germany; (4) the ineluctable impact of global technology and communications, replacing nation-states with both larger and smaller networks; (5) the devolution of power from over-centralised government in London to the various regional assemblies of Edinburgh, Cardiff and Belfast; and, finally, (6) the ultimate acknowledgement, with the passing away of the Princess of Wales, that Royal Britannia is well and truly deceased and that its former subjects now comprise a multi-ethnic, multi-cultural, multi-confessional community no longer seduced by the story of an eternally perduring sovereignty.[9]

The break-up of Britain was as inevitable as it was overdue. So much so that the enormous out-pouring of grief at Diana's demise in 1997 was mourning not just for a particular person but for an entire imperial nation. And curiously the Princess's death was soon reinterpreted as a story of sanctity and sacrifice, her image appearing alongside the image of Mother Teresa of Calcutta (who died within weeks of her) on the streets of London. The Stranger and the Saint reunited in death, under the caption 'Memory of Royalty and Holiness'.

If Ireland was one of the first co-authors of the narrative of the British *natio*, as I have suggested, then it is equally present at its signing off. Ireland is the unsettling vice-narrator in the last chapter of the Kingdom's story, called 'Ulster'. A prompter in the wings for the final denouement of Britannia's royal plot. John Bull's estranged voice echoing back to the mainland. The ultimate 'alienation device' in the drama of split nations.

Nine

America, like all other nations, has defined itself by telling stories of itself and its 'others'. Today, in the aftermath of World Wars and Cold Wars, America has begun to rediscover hidden divisions *within* the national body politic and is responding by inventing new narratives of the alien 'other'. The more extra-terrestrial the better. The postmodern paranoia concerning aliens, running from Hollywood blockbusters, web-site obsessions and cybergames to Reaganite Star War fantasies, is not adventitious. It is, I believe, a telling symptom of mounting millennial hysteria: a symptom informing the current wave of identity-questions – who are we? What is our nation?

Such crises of *identity* are inseparable from a crisis of *legitimisation*. Though a global phenomenon, it is especially acute, I believe, in the Western world, and nowhere more so than in the 'cultural unconscious' of the Western world – America.[1] But what, we may ask, are Americans to aliens and aliens to Americans that they should lose sleep over each other? Let's begin at the beginning.

ONE: THE *MAYFLOWER* MYTH – SAINTS AND STRANGERS

In 1620 a boatload of Pilgrims arrived in Cape Cod. Half of them were separatist Puritans ('Saints'). The other half were non-religious adventurers called 'troublemakers' or

'Strangers'. Saints and Strangers alike had left England because they felt, for different reasons, alienated from their native land. They had become aliens in their own kingdom. It was an inclement December, and the only way to survive when they landed in Massachusetts, feeling threatened by cold, hunger, disease and Indians, was to form a 'communal identity'. The famous Mayflower Compact followed. 'The light of this [one candle] will spread out to our whole country', wrote William Bradford, one of the original founders of New England. Thus, on the basis of a legal tract, the Strangers were integrated with the Saints. Both were illumined by a common Puritan enlightenment extending its rays into the forested dark. The Plymouth Brethren became a united 'us' because they were not 'them' – the primitive savages surrounding them. Within years the skull of the beheaded Metacom, the vanquished Indian leader, hung from the fort of Plymouth, where it remained for two decades, his wife and children sold into slavery in the West Indies. In this primal scene, to be acted out repeatedly over subsequent centuries, identity was constructed over and against difference, the nation forged from a purging of adversaries. New England wasn't Puritan for nothing. Its very foundation was linked to an act of sacrificial purgation – a segregation of pure from impure. The nation was, from the outset, linked to a story of alien-nation.

When the Mayflower first sailed from Plymouth, it might well have taken an alternative route. It could well have tacked eastwards and followed the precedent of the medieval 'ship of fools' (navis stultifera), which for centuries had sailed from one European port to another, offering a spectacle of exotic oddness and otherness to the settled communities on land, reminding them that they were 'normal' after all. The inhabitants of the coastal towns would provide the aliénés on board with goods and provisions in exchange for entertainment.[2] But they made sure not to permit them on shore.

But the *Mayflower* did not sail east. It took a westward route which brought its exiled charges to a place where they could redefine themselves as 'normal', reinventing England in New England, and expelling the natives they found there to a 'savage exteriority' from which there would be no return. Condemned as misfits and monsters by the Established Church and society of fifteenth-century England, the Plymouth Brethren managed to find new misfits and monsters in the New World whom they could in turn condemn. (This phenomenon of fantasising and demonising the New World enemy we might call 'Occidentalism' in counterpoint to Said's 'Orientalism').

The story of inaugural estrangement, thus transposed from *within* the Plymouth Brethren to the indigenous American people *outside* the plantation, was to provide an imaginary solution to the real problem of political division that had plagued the Brethren in their native England. But imaginary solutions were never more than provisional, given the uncanny capacity of the real to reinscribe itself in the plots of history. And so new narratives were called for to sustain the illusion that the descendants of the Pilgrims were *all* Saints, and those of non-Pilgrim stock – e.g. the Indians and, later, the African slaves – were *all* Strangers. This labour of narrative stereotyping began as early as the missionary portraits of the Jamestown Indians in the seventeenth century and was reinforced by hysterical fantasies of demonic possession (for example the Salem witch hunt) and racist demonisation; only to be sustained subsequently by many 'collective stories' over the centuries reaching down to such Hollywood blockbusters as D. W. Griffith's *The Birth of a Nation* (1915) and John Ford's *Stagecoach* (1939).[3]

Thanksgiving remains the US national feast-day, but most Americans today probably do not recall that the turkeys consumed by the Plymouth Brethren at the first celebration of that feast four hundred years ago were provided by local Indians who would have been exterminated or sold into slavery within a matter of years. Most are also probably unaware that over ten million Indian people inhabited America when the Puritans first landed – scarcely a tenth of that figure exist today (1.4 million); or that these natives possessed over 75 per cent of US land up to two hundred years ago and less than 2 per cent today; or that they spoke more languages than were spoken in Europe then or now; or that they signed over 371 legal treaties with the US government between 1778 and 1871, most of which were ignored or traduced. But the question of the Indian stranger within the nation has not gone away. Today many of the tribes are forming sovereignty movements which, as Fergus Bordewich notes in *Killing the White Man's Indian*, are creating 'a hodgepodge of economically and perhaps politically unliveable states whose role is glaringly undefined in the US Constitution'.[4] The return of the repressed serves here as a reminder that there are masked nations within the nation – and that every nation has its hidden tales to tell.

TWO: *THE BIRTH OF A NATION* – A BLACK AND WHITE STORY

This film was premiered in Los Angeles in 1915 and could be said to mark the birth of a certain American film-nation called Hollywood. The director, D. W. Griffith, was a typical product of his time – a white southern racist gentleman – and he had no compunction about initially calling the film *The Clansman*.

On screen, Ku Klux Klansmen in full regalia are seen pursuing perfidious blacks (white actors with make-up); while off-screen these same robed militiamen were present to publicise the opening in Los Angeles.

Griffith's own grandfather had fought on the Confederate side in the Civil War, and this influenced his reactionary portrayal of the War and reconstruction, especially the emancipation of blacks. Ethnic stereotypes fill the screen from genial mammies, Sambos and picaninnies *before* the War to untrustworthy coons and masked brutes *after* the War. This difference is aptly captured in the contrast between the ante-bellum scene of the carefree slaves jigging and singing on the plantation after a twelve-hour shift of cotton-picking and the post-bellum scene of the cruel careerist Lynch packing the formerly white assembly with his uncouth, shoeless fellow blacks; or again in the scene of the freed slave, Gus, pursuing the hapless white heroine to her death. Both Lynch and Gus were played by whites, it being assumed that blacks could not act. This was a black and white minstrel show with a more than sinister twist.

'The task I am trying to achieve', proclaimed Griffith, 'is above all to make you *see*'. And in this film we find an excellent example of how innovative cinematic narration could be used to *screen* – in the double sense of showing and masking – the black-and-white story of the American imaginary. *The Birth of a Nation* was one of the first ever full-length motion pictures (it was three hours long, compared to most previous one-reel Nickelodeon films of ten minutes), and broke away from inherited stage conventions to include full-blown scenes of crowd action, outdoor landscape and even symbolic montage. Griffith invented much of the 'film grammar' – such as cross-cut and close-up – deployed by film-makers; and so doing, he basically jump-started the American motion-picture industry, narrating in the process a deeply prejudicial story of black and white history. The Birth of a Nation was also, interestingly, the first film ever to be screened at the White House.

Griffith used a powerful mix of historical realism and fictional invention for his ideological purposes. For example, he reconstructed Lincoln's assassination in 1865 and Lee's surrender at Appomattox with exemplary exactitude; and he based one of the central characters of the film, Austin Stoneman, on a real-life senator called Thaddeus Stevens, including details of clubfoot and wig. To this Griffith added quotations from historical documents such as the Declaration of Independence, giving the impression that what we were 'seeing' was history *as it actually happened.*

Anticipating hostility from minority quarters, Griffith inserted the following statement into the script: 'We do not fear censorship . . . but we do demand as right, the liberty to show the dark side of wrong, that we may illuminate the bright side of virtue . . .' (Another light/dark metaphor of the white-versus-black message!) And Griffith goes on to claim that his right as artistic narrator to recount truth is a sacrosanct liberty that 'we owe to the Bible and the works of Shakespeare'. Rhetorical echoes of New England Puritanism resound throughout the film.

The basic narrative revolves around two wealthy white families – the Stonemans from the North and the Camerons from the South – tragically separated by a war fought for a meaningless cause (the abolition of slavery). The blacks are the villains of the piece, coming between these two noble branches of WASP stock – epitomised in the sub-plot by the lovers, Elsie Stoneman and Klansman Ben Cameron. The main obstacle to their blessed union comes in the guise of the ruthless black leader, Lynch (whose name masks the fact that 'lynching' was historically perpetrated by *whites against blacks!*) Lynch is shown trying to undermine his benevolent white protector, Senator Stoneman, in order to set up a supremacist 'Negro Nation' and ravish the innocent Elsie Stoneman. The stigmatisation of the upwardly mobile Negro through propaganda inversions of this kind is symptomatic of the scapegoating strategies of white southerners to overcome class divisions amongst themselves by uniting against what was popularly known in Virginia and elsewhere as 'our internal foe' – the Negro. This common black enemy, as one historian put it, was considered a 'sinister being of an alien and "inferior" race who if liberated would bring about social chaos and racial catastrophe'.[5] Slavery in the South was always more than a labour question; it was a way for whites, with slaves or not, to enjoy a sense of racial superiority and control over the 'other' in their midst.

Griffith's crescendo sequence of Klansmen riding to the rescue of 'innocent' whites-about-to-be-lynched, to the accompaniment of Wagner's 'Ride of the Valkyries', is particularly sinister in the light of the subsequent Nazi association of this music with Aryan supremacism – a fact of which Coppola could not have been unmindful when he cited it in the famous GI helicopter attack on the Vietcong village in *Apocalypse Now*.

Interestingly, one of the Klansmen riding to the rescue in *The Birth of a Nation* was none other than John Ford, pioneer of the cowboy-and-Indian 'Western' about to emerge as the dominant Hollywood genre.

THREE: *STAGECOACH* – OUTLAW AND INDIAN

John Ford's *Stagecoach* epitomises how the West was won for the American nation. And reading between the frames, we soon realise that we are here witnessing another rerun of the old *Mayflower* story. Only the western frontier of the New World has now moved further west.

The film tells the tale of an outlaw, Ringo (John Wayne), who undergoes a crisis of legitimisation and identity. Is the convict-cowboy really a criminal or in fact a true defender of law and order? The handcuffed prisoner of the beginning of the story evolves through a series of encounters with alien Indians in the Arizona-Mexican desert to become a law-abiding, happily married man. The telling factor here is that it is the attack by Geronimo's 'savages' that reunites an initially divided group of stagecoach passengers – the stagecoach itself serving as a twentieth-century reworking of the *Mayflower*. The external threat posed by belligerent Indians and unreliable Hispanics along the Arizona border is enough to overcome conflicts of class, sex and legitimacy within the white community. Thanks to the frontier ordeals they endure in no man's land – as they travel for a perilous period unprotected by state cavalry – the sheriff is reconciled with the outlaw, the shunned prostitute with the child-bearing officer's wife, the drunken doctor with the sobering forces of good society. In short, the internal divisions of a community, polarised between Saints and Strangers like the original passengers of the Pilgrim Ship, are ultimately superseded by a new consensus, soldered by the external Indian menace and sealed by the final acts of: (a) homecoming (to the safety and security of the Cavalry fort), (b) child-birth (assisted by the prostitute and reformed doctor) and (c) marriage (between cowboy and prostitute turned-good).

Stagecoach may be viewed, accordingly, as a national rite of passage which traverses the liminal-transitional space between law and non-law. It re-enacts the crises of community and legality at the root of the American nation and resolves them – in terms of the collective *imaginary* – through a series of internal solidarities and integrations in response to a common adversary: the Indians. Ford restages the primal scene of foundational crisis and replays the constitution of American national unity. He 'screens' the return of the suppressed alien, as unconscious origin of community, making the invisible visible – but not so visible that the screening process itself is exposed. Ford shows us how the West was won and the United States became united once again!

In short, in this typical drama of cowboys-and-Indians, the 'strangers' within the stagecoach are reintegrated with the 'saints' against the threat of new *external* 'strangers' – Geronimo and his Apache savages: Metacom's descendants.

FOUR: *MEN IN BLACK* – THE ALIENS ARE COMING

The founding story of Saints and Strangers haunts the New World still, and nowhere more visibly than in the *cultural imaginary*, where games of US (nationals) versus THEM (aliens) are still played out on the country's media screens and Internet sites. A whole series of 'alien' films have been riveting popular attention, from TV serials like the *X-Files* and *Star Trek* to Hollywood blockbusters like *Mars Attacks*, *Independence Day*, the *Star Wars* and *Alien* series and *Men in Black*.[6] The 'aliens' who feature in these movies, and proliferate on the growing number of web-sites devoted to extra-terrestrials, go by such exotic names as 'Greys', 'Nordics', 'Reptoids', 'Chupas', 'MIBs', 'Reptilians' and, tellingly, 'Men in Black'.

In Barry Sonnenfeld's cult movie *Men in Black* – which will

serve as my third cinematic example of US/THEM narratives –
we are treated to an intriguing opening sequence. Illegal
aliens – that is, Hispanic workers or 'wetbacks' – are being
smuggled across the Mexican border into the United States. A
group of Secret Service agents dressed in black suits is moni-
toring this unlawful immigration trail. At one point they hit
upon a suspicious-looking transit vehicle – a reincarnation of
the *Mayflower* and the stagecoach – transporting a cargo of
illegal 'non-resident aliens'. But on proceeding to arrest
them, they discover that they are actually extra-terrestrial aliens
in disguise!

The film proceeds on a roller-coaster ride of twists and
turns with the law-and-order Men in Black (MIB Agents
K and J) seeking out their non-human counterparts. Not only
do both the MIB 'saints' and extra-terrestrial 'strangers' bear
the same name – 'Men in Black' – but they also play the same
role (as secret agents, albeit on opposite sides). And the
viewer is hard put at times to know which exactly is which.
There is even a typical family scene where a farmer goes out to
the yard to check out a noise, only to return to his wife some
time later looking just like himself but somehow changed:
within minutes of his return to the house his whole face and
body begin to disintegrate as an alien creature convulses his
skin. This scene epitomises the alien-nation phenomenon in
that it provokes a paranoid fear that it may well be those most
familiar to us who are secretly most foreign – in this instance,
those who harbour the 'villainous bug' from outer space
which is sent to destroy the all-American apple-pie home,
and by extension New York City itself.

Indeed, this scenario is emblematic of the alien hysteria
replicated in a number of other films, most graphically in *The
Astronaut's Wife*, where the alien virus enters the astronaut's

body during a mysterious space mission and then migrates from him into his wife's womb ('Spencer is inside me', the violated Julianne says of her alienated spouse); or again in *Alien*, where Lieutenant Ripley, a 'saintly' officer played by Sigourney Weaver, is invaded by an extra-terrestrial 'stranger' who grows inside her and eventually bursts out through her torso in the climactic scene of the film. In all three − *Men In Black*, *The Astronaut's Wife* and the *Alien* series − it is telling that the extra-terrestrial reproduces itself by invading a human womb. In the first film, an invaded woman (whose husband is exposed as a 'resident alien' with two identities) gives birth to a tentacled monster in the back of a car; in the second, the astronaut's wife gives birth to alien twins; and in the third, Agent Ripley gives birth to both human and monster off-spring. This 'undecidable' or 'doppelganger' character of the alien–human progeny is itself a perfect illustration of the 'return of the repressed' as a disorienting mix of the biological and the mechanical, the real and the robotic.

It is curious how these films, and related alien movies like *Predator*, *Bladerunner*, *Alien Nation* and *Virus*, operate on such border-lines between human and inhuman − a fuzzy frontier-zone typical of the unconscious phenomenon of the 'uncanny' so central to paranoia and phobia. It is interesting, moreover, that in the making of the *Alien* series the special-effect engineers were requested to make the alien creatures more 'human-like' lest they proved unrecognisable and unbelievable to the viewer − hence the device of the mouth within the mouth: at once monstrous and anthropoid. And a similar effect is produced in *Virus*, where the invisible alien intelligence, transmitted from outer space via (interestingly) a Russian spaceship, contrives to recreate itself in the guise of semi-human, semi-cybernetic beings. The trick in these instances is to create the effect of puppet-like automatons that are also capable of passing as humans.

That *Men in Black* opens with a border-crossing is symptomatic of the whole alien syndrome. Borders have always been favourite places for alien invasions – of the immigrant, adversarial or extra-terrestrial kind. The Rio Grande in particular has long been a borderland of much contention between Latino immigrants and the American government, a conflict zone made even more conflictual in recent years by a growing number of legal disputes concerning the Pueblo Indians, who have started to reclaim ancient territorial rights. It is also along this same southern frontier that most sightings of extra-terrestials and UFOs have occurred. Roswell, Area 51 and other controversial sites of 'alien' landings are located in this no man's land between America and its 'other'.

My basic hypothesis, as I trust is now clear, is that crises of national identity seek provisional resolution by displacing the internal conflict of US/THEM onto an external screen. Hence the recurring need to identify outside enemies – in the interests of national security – which usually goes by the name of *war*. This century, communists, fascists, Cubans, North Koreans, Vietcong and Iraqis have played leading roles in the screening of the 'enemy' without. But these roles have been largely played out. And since there do not appear to be enough spies, subversives or criminals to put on national trial, one tends to note a resurgence of traumas *internal* to the body politic. Examples of this may be witnessed, as noted, in the repetition of Afro-American and Native-American primal scenes; but in order to distract the 'People' from such inner alien-nations and divisions, pretending that there is just one single nation after all, it becomes necessary to exteriorise the enemy again. And if there are no obvious candidates, one has to construct them. Hence the need to de-territorialise aliens, to see them as extra-terrestrial, as coming to us from outer space, invading our homes, abducting our loved ones, penetrating both our minds and our bodies. (One of the key signs of alien abduction is the ominous 'anal probe' – as even the national icon Homer Simpson recently realised!)

The recurring scene of alien-nation also finds expression in media other than film, as an issue of the pop comic *Captain America* published in June 2000 graphically illustrates. Before a nationally broadcast assembly of loyal flag-waving citizens, Captain America announces that he has some 'dire news' which will 'rock the NATION'. His message, received in shock horror by families across the country glued to their TVs, is the following:

> For over two hundred years, we have taught our children that our country has successfully defended its shores against ALL HOSTILE STRIKES. We are mistaken. We have been the victims of a MASSIVE ALIEN INVASION . . . of HORRIFYING PROPORTIONS. Systematically America has been invaded by an alien race bent on earth's destruction. They have taken our PLACES . . . DISGUISED themselves as OUR KIND . . . and now they lie in HIDING, lie in WAIT. . . . Today, with the FULL TRUST of the AMERICAN PEOPLE BEHIND me . . . I have come forward to EXPOSE them before it is TOO LATE! The TRUTH is THIS: ONE OUT OF EVERY TWENTY PEOPLE IN AMERICA is secretly a SKRULL.

And lest we have any doubts about their covert and nefarious operations, Captain America offers a blunt reminder, provoking widespread panic. 'Skrulls hide among us', he warns, 'and we must expose them all before they attack! We must protect our families – our children! They could be anywhere . . . and anyone. Anyone who is different. Who looks out of place. Who isn't like you. . . . They are the enemy. . . . It's US or THEM.'

Now, while such caricature seems innocuous between the covers of a comic, the national psychosis of US/THEM takes on a sinister significance in the light of Ronald Reagan's 'Star War' fantasies or remarks to the effect that invasion from outer space will reunite us all as a community. (On 21 September 1987, Reagan stated to the 42nd General Assembly of the United Nations his firm belief that 'if we were facing an alien threat from outside this world' our differences 'would vanish'.) This point is, moreover, cleverly cited in the cult film *Alien Nation* when a spacecraft full of 'newcomers' lands in a southern US landscape, while locals in a bar wonder why the aliens couldn't have chosen Russia instead as they glare up at a TV monitor broadcasting Reagan's famous Star Wars speech.

Such propaganda becomes more sinister still, however, when placed in the context of the characteristically xenophobic speech made by the Reform Party presidential candidate Pat Buchanan, just months before the *Captain America* cartoon was published. The following extracts, broadcast on the Web, give an idea of how fear of the foreign can migrate from extra-terrestrial to immigrant aliens (and back again) with disturbing ease: 'There are five million illegal aliens here', thunders Buchanan. 'It is a near-certainty that enemies of this country have seeded that population with agents – for purposes of espionage, terror, assassination or reprisal. . . . Ours are the most porous borders on Earth. . . . Our European ethnic core – 90% in 1965 – is shrinking fast.' So he asks: 'How much "diversity" can we tolerate before we cease to be one nation and one people? What do we have in common anymore?' Then the mask drops altogether. 'We see the troubling signs of a national turning away from the idea that we are *one* people and the emergence of a radically different idea, that we are *separate* ethnic nations within a nation.' By way of responding to this alien threat, Buchanan promises that as President he will 'halt illegal immigration by securing our porous borders and strengthening internal enforcement' (2 March 1999).

Such tales of enemies invading the US homeland are not, of course, unprecedented in American presidential campaigns – Nixon made much of reds-at-the-border fears, and the tele-evangelist Pat Robertson, who ran for the Republican nomination in 1988, even spoke of a satanic conspiracy of foreigners (largely Jewish and Masonic 'illuminati') who threatened the true 'Christian Coalition' at the heart of the United States. But such right-wing propaganda assumes particularly disturbing proportions in the context of George W. Bush's determination to press ahead with the National Missile Defense System (NMDS). To glean public support for this move, a powerful lobby calling itself the Coalition to Protect Americans Now has set up a web-site which includes a zip-code-based 'Missile Threat Calculator': below the picture of an all-American family home with garden and of mother embracing children, one can enter one's personal zip code to establish exactly how 'vulnerable one is to missile attack'. A Customised Missile Threat Profile displays the risks of attack from at least sixteen different types of missiles from China, Iran, Russia and other 'rogue nations' (all visualisable on a global map). But the biggest rogue nation of all – once wars are extra-territorialised in this way and relocated in outer space – is the nation of extra-terrestrials themselves! At least at the level of the unconscious imaginary where popular paranoia does most of its fancywork.

And yet the official Republican story is very different. Just listen to George W. Bush's Inauguration speech of January 2001: 'We have a place all of us, in a long story . . . the story of the new world that became a friend of the old. The story of a slave-holding society that became a servant of freedom. The story of a power that went into the world to protect but not possess, to defend but not to conquer. It is the American story . . .'. Between official and unofficial stories there is clearly a conflict of interpretations. Democracy has the daunting task of working through such conflict.

Conclusion: Border Crossings
Ten

The recurrence of the primal scene of Saint and Stranger is, in sum, what the current obsession with aliens is really all about. That is why I've been suggesting that films like *Men in Black* and the seemingly endless *Star Wars* and *Alien* series (the first of which was released in the wake of the Iran hostage crisis) so captivate the American national unconscious.[1] Why presidential Star War fantasies are taken extremely seriously even when they seem to defy normal distinctions between reality and fiction. Why films like *Wag the Dog*, exposing the diversionary need for far-flung overseas enemies, tap the pulse of America's unspoken legitimisation crisis. Why court dramas like the O. J. Simpson or Rodney King cases are played out with compulsive repetitiveness on national screens, reminding citizens that the one frail thing which binds them together – besides the dollar, the Superbowl and the TV weathermap – is a legal document, the Constitution.[2]

But the Constitution which acknowledges all Americans as *one* is itself fractured, like the Bell of Liberty Hall in Philadelphia where it was drafted, to the extent that it is founded on the forgetfulness of originary violence – against native Indians and abducted slaves in particular. And that explains too, perhaps, the almost obsessional references to court-room tribunals in American televisual and cinematic culture – expressing the need, as it were, to fill in the cracks, to redraw the lines between law and outlaw, to persuade its citizens that the Nation really is legitimate, constitutional, descended from Puritan Pilgrims and even purer Founding Fathers. (This act of persuasion is what Max Weber calls the 'charismatic' function of power, which supplements the power of administrative government, especially when it risks loosing legitimacy at a collective level.) There are in fact many dividing lines zig-zagging through the American story, like the one drawn in sand at the Alamo, or along the Mason–Dixon border, or across the banks of the Rio Grande – that US/Mexican bound-ary which, as noted, aliens have made their favourite landing site and which Hispanics and Pueblo Indians trespass with increasing defiance. Aliens always flourish in border country.[3]

Creatures which hang around borders, and disrespect their integrity, are traditionally known as 'monsters'. They comprise a species of sinister miscreants exiled from the normative categories of the established system. A species of non-species, as it were. Alien monsters represent the 'unthought' of any given point of knowledge and representa-tion, the unfamiliar spectre which returns to haunt the secure citadel of consciousness. 'There are monsters on the prowl', writes Michel Foucault, 'whose form changes with the history of knowledge.'

This echoes the Nietzschean view that the 'monstrous' is a synonym of 'the strange, the exotic, the crooked, the self-contradictory'; and it exposes so-called aliens as those who defy conventional categories of 'true and false propositions' and 'push a whole teratology of knowledge back beyond its margins'.[4] On this account, the alien is the Other 'conceived of in a double that is taken for a single form'. It is that strange and estranging dimension of experience often deemed 'unnatural', 'denatured' or 'vomited by nature'. And for this very reason it is considered a treachery to our political and social norms.[5] Even Marx spoke of the 'spectre of communism'. In short, aliens, strangers and monsters are denounced as an offence against both nature and reason – symptoms, if you will, of 'epistemic illegitimacy'. The regulating force of official discourse tries to keep monstrosity at bay, writes Andrew Gibson in 'Narrative and Monstrosity', 'wards it off as a dismaying or inadmissible threat. Monstrosity, in fact – and not error – is what most menaces the will to truth, because it is radically heterogeneous to and cannot be accommodated by that will.' Monsters are therefore ostracised as 'mad' by the guardians of conventional Sanity, Identity, Legality and Normalcy. Whence the not surprising conclusion that 'monstrosity is the otherness that undermines any concept of man as unitary, knowable being'.[6] Of course, for Foucault, Gibson and certain other neo-Nietzschean commentators, monsters are to be celebrated rather than demonised. There is even a growing number of New Age religious groups who believe that the ultimate alien is none other than God! (The Raelian religion, for example, proclaims that 'extraterrestials are the true face of God'.)[7]

But while all this talk of aliens and monsters may appear fanciful, it is sobering to recall that a *Life* magazine poll, published in March 2000, shows a majority of Americans believing in the existence of aliens, and over 30 per cent claiming that aliens have made landings in the United States (2,416 sightings were reported in 1999 alone). Two million US citizens say that they have personally met one. So, if God is indeed to save America, as the anthem says, he could surely do no better than send more alien spaceships to distract its citizens from the aliens within themselves.

I would suggest, finally, that philosophy might try to address such contemporary psychodramas of inclusion and exclusion, in America and elsewhere, by questioning dogmatic polarisations between US and THEM – that is, by challenging the binary opposition separating ourselves as 'saints' from others as 'strangers'. For while 'saints' and 'strangers' are not always the same, they are not always diametrically opposed either. There is probably a 'saint' in most 'strangers' and a 'stranger' in most 'saints'. Philosophy might help us discern a little better and make more sensitive and just judgements where possible.[8]

Part Four
Narrative Matters

Eleven

There are three points about stories: if told, they like to be heard; if heard, they like to be taken in; and if taken in, they like to be told.

Ciaran Carson, **Fishing For Amber: A Long Story**[1]

There has been much talk as we pass into the third millennium that we have reached the end of the story. I am not just referring to the usual millennial fantasies of apocalypse and anarchy, but to a general sentiment of slackening and senselessness. The old Master Narratives – of Judaeo–Christian redemption, Revolutionary Liberation or Enlightenment Progress – are for many no longer engaging Western imagination and belief. And it is in this climate that we find frequent talk of the 'end of history' (Fukuyama), coinciding with pronouncements about the 'end of ideology' (Bell) and the 'end of the story' (Baudrillard; or from a positivist perspective, Hempel).

By contrast, when someone like Walter Benjamin talked about a radical threat to the power of narrativity in our expanding information age, he did not, I believe, mean the end of storytelling *per se*. He was merely signalling the imminent demise of certain forms of remembrance which presupposed age-old traditions of inherited experience, seamlessly transmitted from one generation to the next. This indeed has come to an end. We can hardly deny that the notion of continuous experience, associated with traditional linear narrative, has been fundamentally challenged by current technologies of the computer and Internet. Nor can we ignore the evidence of a society where hyper-advanced tele-communications and digital data flows have begun replacing the old mnemonic, epistolary and print modes of expression. Our inherited notions of rooted space and time are being profoundly altered by the emerging megapolis of expanding velocity and immediacy – giving rise to what some regard as an increasingly deterritorialised world.[2]

None of this can be denied. But we can, I believe, question the verdict of some that we have reached, on that account, the end of the story. Storytelling will never end, for there will always be someone to say 'Tell me a story', and somebody else who will respond 'Once upon a time ... '. To be sure, the old stories are giving way to new ones, more multi-plotted, multi-vocal and multi-media. And these new stories are often, as we know, truncated or parodied to the point of being called micro-narratives or post-narratives. Some are even told *backwards*, like Martin Amis's *Time's Arrow*; or recounted in several simultaneous storylines, like Mike Figgis's digitally shot film *Timecode*, where four separate feature-length takes occupy the screen throughout, allowing multiple narratives to overlap and criss-cross. But such innovative experiments are *still* linked to the extended narrative family, as prodigal sons are linked to forebears (*mythos-mimesis*) who keep some lines of communication, however tenuous, open.

So when a group of *nouveaux-romanciers* began to declare in the 1960s and 1970s that 'the story as such must be obliterated', I think that they had a very specific notion of the old classic realist novel in mind. One only has to read their moratorium on narrative to see what a restricted vision of storytelling they were targeting:

all the technical elements of the narrative . . . the
unconditional adoption of chronological development, linear
plots, a regular graph of the emotions, the way each episode
tended towards an end, etc. . . . everything aimed at imposing
the image of a stable universe, coherent, continuous, univocal
and wholly decipherable.[3]

Granted. But we didn't need Parisian literati to tell us this. The
Dubliner James Joyce had told us as much decades earlier
when he revolutionised the whole storytelling process with
daring new experiments in fictional narration. The simple fact
that story-forms mutate from age to age does not mean that
they disappear. They just change their 'habitation and their
name'. Indeed, one could even claim that the urge of certain
literary obituarists to declare the end of the story is, ironically,
a continuing sign of the *need* for traditional narrative closure
(what Kermode calls the 'sense of an ending'). So when
someone like Robbe-Grillet claims that 'novels that contain
characters belong well and truly to the past', it is more likely
to be his novels that belong to the past. Just as when Roland
Barthes announces that 'in narrative no-one speaks', it is
Barthes himself who belies his own statement – in a typical
performative contradiction – by inventing a narrative about
the end of narrative and signing his own authorial name,
qua narrator, to this story. (He also presumably collected his
royalties and safeguarded the copyright of this same
'no-one'.)

I do not wish to be facetious, merely to issue a wager that
storytelling will survive the suspicions cast upon it by apocalyptic anti-humanists, no less than by positivists like Carl
Hempel or structuralists of the *annales* school who believe that
the historical sciences should divest themselves of all narrative

functions in deference to objective norms and codes. The stubborn resistance to narrativity in the name of reductive models of scientism will, I am convinced, soon yield to the awareness that historical truth is as much the property of 'narrative knowledge' as it is of so-called 'objective knowledge'. There is more to the science of history than the methods of empirico-metrics and structural logics ever dreamed of.

In terms of recent controversies, I personally endorse the affirmative view of narrativity advanced by theorists like Ricoeur, Taylor, Rorty, MacIntyre or Nussbaum. Or indeed by more popular authors like Christopher Vogler, author of *The Writer's Journey*, who argues that the advent of cyber-culture should be seen not as a threat to storytelling but as a catalyst for new possibilities of interactive, non-linear narration. The fact is that no matter how much technologies transform our modes of storytelling, people will always 'enjoy going into a story trance and allowing themselves to be led through a tale by a masterful story weaver'.[4]

In this concluding part, then, I would like to throw down the gauntlet and champion the irrepressible art of the story. I propose to do so under five summary headings, each deriving from the earliest attempt by Western philosophy to formulate a model for narrative, namely, Aristotelian poetics. The five headings are as follows: plot (*mythos*), re-creation (*mimesis*), release (*catharsis*), wisdom (*phronesis*), and ethics (*ethos*). I shall take each in turn with a view to retrieving and rethinking these enduring functions of storytelling in the light of contemporary hermeneutic readings. So doing, I shall endeavour to bring the most ancient of theories into critical dialogue with their most cutting-edge counterparts today.

ONE: PLOT (*MYTHOS*)

Every human existence is a life in search of a narrative. This is not simply because it strives to discover a pattern to cope with the experience of chaos and confusion. It is also because each human life is *always already* an implicit story. Our very finitude constitutes us as beings who, to put it baldly, are born at the beginning and die at the end. And this gives a temporal structure to our lives which seek some kind of *significance* in terms of referrals back to our past (memory) and forward to our future (projection). So that we might say that our lives are constantly interpreting themselves – pre-reflectively and pre-consciously – in terms of beginnings, middles and ends (though not necessarily in that order). In short, our existence is already to some extent pre-plotted before we ever consciously seek out a narrative in which to reinscribe our life as life-history.

Aristotle was one of the first philosophers to identify this pre-narrative pattern to the extent that he realised that human existence is a life of 'action' and that action is always conducted *in view of some end* – even if that end is itself. In other words, as human agents we are always prefiguring our world in terms of an inter-active life with others. The work of *mythos*, as defined in the *Poetics*, gives a specific grammar to this life of action by transposing it into (1) a telling; (2) a fable or fantasy; and (3) ·a crafted structure. All three meanings of *mythos* convey the common function of narrative as *poiesis*: that is, a way of *making* our lives into life-stories. This is always already at work in our everyday existence, but it only becomes explicit when transposed into the poetic genres of tragedy, epic or comedy (the three recognised by Aristotle).

Augustine internalised this narrative structure as an interplay of dispersal and integration within the soul itself. The former he called *distentio animi*, attributing it to our fallen nature evinced in the scattering of the self over past, present and future. The latter integrating function he ascribed to the contervailing movement of the psyche towards identity over time (*intentio animi*). The resulting drama between these two tendencies results in a tension between discordance and concordance that makes each life a temporal plot in search of an ultimate author – for Augustine, God.

Picking up on this proto-existential description of human emplotment and temporality, twentieth-century phenomenologists found different ways of reformulating this narrative drama: Husserl called it the internal time-consciousness of retention and protention; Heidegger the temporal circle of retrieval (*Wiederholung*) and project (*Entwurf*) in the light of our 'being towards an end' – namely, our 'being-towards-death'; Gadamer called it the 'anticipation of completion' that organises my existence as a whole; and Ricoeur, the prefigurative 'synthesis of the heterogeneous'. Our contemporary phenomenology recognises that narrativity is what marks, organises and clarifies temporal experience; and that every historical process is recognised as such to the degree that it can be recounted. A story is made out of events, and the plot (*mythos*) is what mediates between events and the story.[5]

But the most important point to bear in mind is that from the Greek discovery of human life (*bios*) as meaningfully interpreted action (*praxis*) to the most recent descriptions of existence as narrative temporality, there is an abiding recognition that existence is inherently storied. Life is pregnant with stories. It is a nascent plot in search of a midwife. For inside every human being there are lots of little narratives trying to get out. 'Human life has a determinate form', as Alasdair MacIntyre explains, 'the form of a certain kind of story. It is not just that poems and sagas narrate what happens to men and women, but that in their narrative form poems and sagas capture a form that was already present in the lives which they relate.'[6]

That is why every person's action can be read as part of an unfolding life-story, and why each life-story cries out to be 'imitated', that is, transformed into the story of a life.

TWO: RE-CREATION (*MIMESIS*)

Mimesis may be seen accordingly as an imaginative redescription which captures what Aristotle called the 'essence' (*eidos*) of our lives. *Mimesis* is not about idealist escapism or servile realism. It is a pathway to the disclosure of the inherent 'universals' of existence that make up human truth (*Poetics* 1451). Far from being a passive copy of reality, *mimesis* re-enacts the real world of action by magnifying its essential traits (1448a). It remakes the world, so to speak, in the light of its potential truths.

The most important thing in our descriptions of the temporality of *mythos* is a latent interweaving of past, present and future (though not necessarily in that order). What distinguishes human action from mere physical movement, we discovered, is that it is always a dynamic *synthesis* of residual sedimentation and future-oriented goals. Every action is directed towards some result that informs and motivates the agent's aim in acting. This is what Dilthey and the hermeneutic thinkers meant when they said that 'life interprets itself' ('das Leben legt sich selber aus'). And it is because of this directedness, conscious or unconscious, that our lives may be described as a flux of events which combine to form an action which is both *cumulative* and *oriented* – two crucial features of any narrative.[7] But while existence may thus be considered as pre-narrative, it is not fully narrative until it is re-created in terms of a formal verbal recounting. Until, that is, the tacit pre-plotting of our temporalising-synthesising existence is structurally emplotted. Until implicit *mythos* becomes explicit *poiesis*. This double move of narrative proper involves a second patterning of our already patterned (symbolically mediated) experience.

This is probably what Aristotle meant when he said that poetic narration is the 'imitation of an action' (*mimesis praxeos*). And I think that we could also give a liberal reading here of his claim that poetic insight comes at that point in a narrative when the protagonist 'recognises again' (*anagnorisis*) the inherent direction of his or her existence – call it fate, fortune, destiny, or the 'divinity that shapes our ends' (*Hamlet*). Mimesis is 'invention' in the original sense of that term: *invenire* means both to discover *and* to create, that is, to disclose what is already there in the light of what is not yet (but is potentially). It is the power, in short, to re-create actual worlds as possible worlds.

This power of mimetic re-creation sustains a connection between fiction and life while also acknowledging their difference. Life can be properly understood only by being retold mimetically through stories. But the act of *mimesis* which enables us to pass from life to life-story introduces a 'gap' (however minimal) between living and recounting. Life is lived, as Ricoeur reminds us, while stories are told. And there is a sense in which the untold life is perhaps less rich than a told one.[8] Why? Because the recounted life prises open perspectives inaccessible to ordinary perception. It marks a poetic extrapolation of possible worlds which supplement and refashion our referential relations to the life-world existing prior to the act of recounting. Our exposure to new possibilities of being refigures our everyday being-in-the world. So that when we return from the story-world to the real world, our sensibility is enriched and amplified in important respects. In that sense we may say that *mimesis* involves both a free-play of fiction *and* a responsibility to real life. It does not force us to make a Yeatsian choice between 'perfection of the life or of the work'.

This brings me, ultimately, to what Ricoeur calls the circle of triple *mimesis*: (1) the *prefiguring* of our life-world as it seeks to be told; (2) the *configuring* of the text in the act of telling; and (3) the *refiguring* of our existence as we return from narrative text to action. This referral of the narrative text back to the life of the author and forward to the life of the reader belies the structuralist maxim that the text relates to nothing but itself. Which is not to deny that life is linguistically mediated; only to say that such mediation always points beyond itself and is not confined to a self-regarding play of signifiers (what Jameson calls the 'prisonhouse of language'). This is why we insist that the act of *mimesis* involves a circular movement from action to text and back again – passing from prefigured experience through narrative recounting back to a refigured life-world.[9] In short, life is always *on the way* to narrative, but it does not arrive there until someone hears and tells this life as a story. Which is why the latent prefiguring of everyday existence calls out for a more formal configuring (*mythos-mimesis*) by narrative texts.

In the light of the above reflections, I prefer to translate *mimesis* with Ricoeur and MacIntyre as a kind of creative retelling, thereby avoiding the connotations of servile representation mistakenly associated with the traditional term 'imitation'. The key to *mimesis* resides in a certain 'gap' demarcating the narrated world from the lived one, opened up by the fact that every narrative is told from a certain point of view and in a certain style and genre. This is especially evident in the case of fiction, where storytelling takes the form of epic, drama, romance, novel or, more recently, such electronic or digital forms as film, video and interactive hypertexts.[10]

In all these forms, the gap separating real life from simulated life-likeness is relatively unmistakable. There are, of course, those who argue for a direct 'causal' rapport between media violence and mounting street violence, for example, but I think that most people recognise when they are passing from the real to the imaginary or back again – without the need for formulas like 'once upon a time' to signal the transition. These things are implied. The rules of poetic licence are generally understood by people sitting in a darkening cinema or theatre, opening the pages of a novel in a room, or listening to someone in a cafe or pub begin a story with the words, 'I tell you no lie . . .' (which in Ireland means the opposite). The bottom line, as the judge in the New York court ruling on Joyce's *Ulysses* said, is that 'no one was ever raped by a book'. To suggest otherwise is not only to underestimate ordinary people's intelligence, but grossly to insult those who experience *real* violence in the *real* world. People just know, and have known since the first palaeolithic caveman said 'I'll tell you a story . . .', that there is a difference between lived and recounted life. And the first civilisation to erode that difference, or our awareness of it, is a civilisation in dire straits.

The question of *mimesis* becomes far more vexed, of course, when it comes to *historical* narratives. But here too, the hiatus between the historical recounting of the past (*historia rerum gestarum*) and the historical past itself (*res gestae*) has almost always been acknowledged. Even though the past can be reconstructed only through narrative imagination, the 'gap' between reality and representation here is of a qualitatively different kind from that operating in fiction. In history-telling we do not enjoy the same poetic licence or 'willing suspension of disbelief' (as Coleridge put it) that operates in fiction. Historical narratives could not function as *history* if there were not some basic *veracity*-claims involved. There is at least here a minimal claim to tell the past as it truly was; if historians are to be taken seriously, their accounts must be credible. In other words, historical narratives, unlike fictional ones, hold that their accounts *refer* to things that actually happened – regardless of how varied and contested the interpretations of what happened may be. The reference can be multiple, split or truncated, but it still sustains a belief in the real events (*genomena*) recounted by the historian. That is why it is so important, for example, to recognise a difference in our attitudes when reading Michelet's historical account of Napoleon and Tolstoy's fictional account in *War and Peace*. (Even though both involve a certain mixing of history and fiction, the former does so as 'imaginative history', the latter as 'historical novel'.) Or to cite a more graphic example, it is vital to observe a distinction between the truth-claims involved in the news story of the Vietcong girl covered in napalm and the tale of the Little Mermaid covered in fish-scales. Once a story is told as history it makes very different claims on the past from those made by fiction.

History and fiction, in sum, both refer to human action, but they do so on the basis of distinct referential claims. Where fiction discloses possible worlds of action, history seeks *grosso modo* to comply with the criteria of evidence common to the general body of science. Ricoeur describes the different truth-claims involved in history and fiction thus:

> In the conventional sense attached to the term 'truth' by the acquaintance with this body of science, only historical knowledge may enunciate its referential claim as a 'truth'-claim. But the very meaning of this truth-claim is itself measured by the limiting network which rules the conventional descriptions of the world. This is why fictional narratives may assert a referential claim of another kind, appropriate to the split reference of poetic discourse. This referential claim is nothing other than the claim to redescribe reality according to the symbolic structures of the fiction.[11]

This is not, of course, to deny that once history is narrated it already assumes certain techniques of 'telling' and 'retelling' that make it more than a reportage of empirical facts. Even the presumption that the past can be told *as* it truly happened still contains the gap of the figural 'as'. History-telling is never literal (*pace* positivists or fundamentalists). It is always at least in part *figurative* to the extent that it involves telling according to a certain selection, sequencing, emplotment and perspective. But it does try to be *truthful*. Were this not the case, there would be no way of countering the historical distortions of Holocaust deniers or propagandists. We would be unable to respect our debts of memory, in particular to the forgotten victims of history. History-telling seeks to address the silences of history by giving a voice to the voiceless. 'The meaning of human existence', as Ricoeur rightly observes, 'is not just the power to change or master the world, but also the ability to be remembered and recollected in narrative discourse.'[12] But this controversial question of narrative truth and memory is something which we shall revisit in section 4 on 'narrative wisdom' (*phronesis*) below.

The mimetic role of narrative, to conclude our present discussion, is never fully absent from *history-telling* even as it is fully present in *fiction-telling*. That is why I am arguing that we shall never reach the end of the story. We shall never arrive at a point, even in our most 'post' of postmodern cultures, where we could credibly declare a moritorium on storytelling. Even postmodern parodies of the narrative imagination like Calvino's *If on a Winter's Night a Traveller* or Beckett's *Imagination Dead Imagine* presuppose the narrative act they are parodying. Think of the titles. Such parodies subvert old modes of telling with alternative ones. The serpent of storytelling may swallow its own tail, but it never disappears altogether.

THREE: RELEASE (CATHARSIS)

Next I want to look at the proposition that stories possess a specifically cathartic power. I mean by this, first, the idea that stories 'alter' us by transporting us to other times and places where we can experience things *otherwise*. This is the power to 'feel what wretches feel', as King Lear put it. To know what it is like to be in someone else's head, shoes or skin. The power, in short, of *vicarious* imagination.

Aristotle defined catharsis as 'purgation by pity and fear'. Let us begin with 'fear' (*phobos*). Aristotle believed that dramatised stories could offer us the freedom to behold all kinds of unpalatable and unliveable events, which by being narrated have some of the harm removed. 'Objects which in themselves we view with pain', he says, 'we delight to contemplate when reproduced with minute fidelity: such as the forms of the most ignoble beasts and of dead animals' (*Poetics* 1448b). We may, he suggests, experience a certain cathartic release from the tragic sufferings of existence in our role of spectators (anticipating the Kantian notion of 'disinterestedness'). Why? Because the very contrivance and artifice of *mimesis* detaches us from the action unfolding before us, affording us sufficient distance to grasp the meaning of it all. This distancing or 'fearful' aspect of catharsis comes from the gap opened up between the literal and the figural by the art of 'imitated action'. It provokes a certain 'awe' (*phobos*) before the workings of fate. It is what we experience in *Oedipus Rex* when we learn the true meaning of the riddle of the Sphinx, or in *Hamlet* when we register the Prince's discovery that there is a 'divinity that shapes our ends'. It is what Stephen Daedalus calls — in his famous account of Aristotelian catharsis in *A Portrait of the Artist as a Young Man* — 'knowledge of the secret cause of things'. Cathartic awe stops us in our tracks, throws us off kilter, deworlds us. The Greeks identified this with the detachment of Olympian deities, enabling us to see through things, however troubling or terrible, to their inner or ultimate meaning.

But that is only half the story. As well as being distanced, we need to be sufficiently *involved* in the action to feel that it matters. Catharsis, as noted, purges us by pity as well as fear. It comprises a double attitude of both empathy and detachment. By pity (*eleos*) the Greeks understood the ability to suffer with others (*sym-pathein*). The narrated action of a drama, for example, solicits a mode of sympathy more extensive and resonant than that experienced in ordinary life. And it does so not simply because it enjoys the poetic licence to suspend our normal protective reflexes (which guard us from pain) but also because it amplifies the range of those we might empathise with — reaching beyond family, friends and familiars to all kinds of foreigners. If we read *Oedipus Rex*, we experience what it is like to be a Greek who murders his father and marries his mother. If we read *Anna Karenina*, we experience the tragic fate of a passionate woman in nineteenth-century Russia. If we read *Scarlet and Black*, we relive the life of an erratic, wilful youth in Napoleonic France. And if we read *The Jaguar* by Ted Hughes, we can even transport ourselves into the skin of a 'non-rational' animal. What is impossible in reality is made possible in fiction.

This power of empathy with living things other than ourselves – the stranger the better – is a major test not just of poetic imagination but of ethical sensitivity. And in this regard we might go so far as to say that genocides and atrocities presuppose a *radical failure of narrative imagination*. Jonathan Swift believed this, for instance, when he wrote *A Modest Proposal* with a view to securing understanding of the Irish Famine in his English readers. And one of J. M. Coetzee's characters, Elizabeth Costello, applies similar arguments to the Holocaust:

> The particular horror of the camps, the horror that convinces us that what went on there was a crime against humanity, is not that despite a humanity shared with their victims, the killers treated them like lice. That is too abstract. The horror is that the killers refused to think themselves into the place of their victims, as did everyone else. They said, 'It is *they* in those cattle-cars rattling past.' They did not say, 'How would it be if it were I in that cattle-car?' They did not say, 'It is I who am in that cattle-car.' They said, 'It must be the dead who are being burnt today, making the air stink and falling in ash on my cabbages.' They did not say, 'How would it be if I were burning?' They did not say, 'I am burning, I am falling in ash.'

In other words, concludes Elizabeth Costello,

they closed their hearts. The heart is the seat of a faculty, *sympathy*, that allows us to share at times the being of another. . . . There are people who have the capacity to imagine themselves as someone else, there are people who have no such capacity, and there are people who have the capacity but choose not to exercise it . . . there is no limit to the extent to which we can think ourselves into the being of another. There are no bounds to the sympathetic imagination.[13]

If we possess narrative sympathy — enabling us to see the world from the other's point of view — we cannot kill. If we do not, we cannot love.

We might say, consequently, that catharsis affords a singular mix of pity and fear whereby we experience the suffering of other beings *as if* we were them. And it is precisely this double-take of difference and identity — experiencing oneself as another and the other as oneself — that provokes a reversal of our natural attitude to things and opens us to novel ways of seeing and being.

One especially moving example of the cathartic narrator is Helen Bamber, and a major reason for this is that she is an exceptionally 'good listener'. Bamber's ability to receive repressed stories and return them to the speakers themselves — and to other listeners and readers — had extraordinary healing results. I have already cited her work of witness in relation to the narratives of Belsen, where she worked as therapist and counsellor after the liberation. But Bamber's work also extended to Amnesty International and its multiple records of testimony to victims of torture throughout the world. One particularly powerful case, reported in *The Good Listener*, is that of Bill Beaushire, a 'disappeared' victim of the Chilean coup against Allende, who suffered the most appalling treatment, including electrocution and repeated hangings, before his eventual execution. The story of Beaushire transmitted by Bamber 'was description, but it was also a way of paying heed to memory', an acknowledgement of the need to have this story 'connected to the world of those who had not been tortured'. The Beaushire dossier would, thanks to her witness, serve as an indispensable testament to an individual's otherwise forgotten fate, 'told in the many voices of those who saw him after he "disappeared" '.[14] As one of the survivors of Chile's terror remarked, 'you never give up on your dead . . . we must *acknowledge* the truth, as well as having knowledge of it'. This double duty of admission and cognition is the irremissible task of narrative remembrance.

A final example of cathartic testimony I would like to cite here is that of a survivor of the Armenian massacre. One evening in the summer of 1915 a young Armenian mother hid her baby in a mulberry bush in the mountain village of Kharpert in eastern Turkey. The child, who survived the subsequent slaughter of the village population by Turkish troops, was Michael Hagopian, who eighty years later completed a documentary film called *Voices from the Lake*. The killing of over 1.5 million Armenians is called the 'silent genocide' since it has always been denied by the Turkish government. Hagopian spent years researching the film, travelling widely to glean first-hand testimonies and stitching together the events which unfolded in that fateful year. One of the most important pieces of evidence was a series of photographs taken by an American diplomat, posted to Turkey at the time, which he buried on his departure from the country for fear they would be confiscated. Many years later he returned and retrieved the photos, faded and gnawed at the edges, but providing proof nonetheless of claims that over 10,000 bodies were deposited in the lake just west of Khapert. This reclaiming of buried 'imitations of an action' served as confirmation of Hagopian's story of genocide, verifying the dictum, 'you can kill a people but you cannot silence their voices' (the *Montreal Gazette*, 22 April 2000, p. 10). In allowing these suppressed voices to speak at last after more than eighty years of silence, Hagopian permits a certain working-through of memory, if by no means a cure. And this is crucial to the whole work of catharsis: it is a matter of acknowledging painful truths – through the 'gap' of narrative imitation – rather than some magic potion which miraculously resolves them. Catharsis is a matter of recognition, not remedy.[15]

What the stories of people like Beaushire, Hagopian or Srebnik demonstrate is that testimonies may serve sympathic imagination as powerfully as fictional ones. Whether it is a matter of history or fiction, *mimesis* imitates action in such a way that we can re-present things absent or forgotten. And this narrative function of making absent things present can serve a therapeutic purpose.

FOUR: WISDOM (*PHRONESIS*)

And so we return to the vexed question: what can we know about the world from stories? Is there a truth proper to fiction? And if so, how does this differ from the truth of history, understood as events worked over by certain story structures but retaining a referential claim to the way things actually happened? Presuming that they do indeed differ, as I have been arguing throughout this book, we might then ask how this relates to the curious fact that the word 'history' in English, as in several other languages (for example *Geschichte, historia, histoire*) means *both* events *and* our narrated accounts of these events. A fact underscored by the canonical definition of *histoire* in the *Dictionnaire universel* as both the 'narration of things as they happened' and a 'fabulous but credible story made up by an author'.[16]

My basic view is that however historical and fictional narratives relate to each other, there *is* a kind of understanding specific to narrativity in general and that this corresponds closely to what Aristotle called *phronesis* – namely, a form of practical wisdom capable of respecting the singularity of situations as well as the nascent universality of values aimed at by human actions. This particular kind of 'phronetic' understanding results from a certain *overlapping* of history and story. It acknowledges that there is always a certain fictionality to our representing history 'as if' we were actually there in the past to experience it (which in reality we weren't). And, by the same token, it recognises a certain historical character to fictional narratives – for example the fact that most stories are recounted in the *past* tense and describe characters and events as though they were *real*. As Aristotle put it, for narrative to work what seems impossible must be made credible (*Poetics* 1460a 26–7). Which is perhaps why even the most inhuman monsters in science-fiction narratives must bear some resemblance to historically life-like beings if they are to be recognised or to command our interest. As already noted, for example, the extra-terrestrials in the *Alien* series have organs, mouths and tails, and even the AI cyber-machine in *2001: A Space Odyssey* carries a human name, Hal, and speaks with a human voice. The question of *literary belief* is absolutely crucial to the working of narrative; for the narrator makes a 'secondary world', and once we enter it we make believe that what is narrated is 'true' in so far as it accords with the laws of that world. 'You believe it, while you are, as it were, inside. The moment disbelief arises, the spell is broken; the magic, or rather art, has failed.'[17]

It is this curious criss-crossing of narrative functions which allows (a) for fiction to portray the 'essential' truths of life that Aristotle speaks of, and (b) for history to portray a credible sense of particularity. But while confirming this interweaving of fiction and history on the arc of narrative, I would equally insist on identifying their different locations on this arc – for example, the former clearly gravitates towards the pole of the 'imaginary', the latter towards that of the 'real'. And I would insist, moreover, that the great majority of readers, including young children, know how to make this primordial distinction.[18] The story of the Frog-King is possible only, as Tolkien reminds us, because we know that frogs are not men and that princesses do not marry them in the real world of history!

There are devil's advocates galore, of course, when it comes to narrative truth. Let me briefly rehearse a number of them by way of clarifying my own position. I have already cited certain constructivists, like Schafer in psychotherapy or Hayden White in history, who espouse a position of pragmatic relativism. Narratives, on this account, are deemed pure linguistic functions with no reliable reference to any truth beyond themselves. They involve a self-referential play of signifiers, spliced together in an intra-textual web.[19] Espousing a postmodern position of Irony, White will admit that this view tends to erode

all belief in positive political actions. In its apprehension of
the essential folly or absurdity of the human condition, it
tends to engender belief in the 'madness' of civilisation itself

and to inspire a Mandarin-like disdain for those seeking to grasp the nature of social reality in either science or art.[20]

White basically argues that because all narrated history is inevitably mediated by linguistic processes of emplotment, explication and ideology, we are somehow obliged to embrace an 'irreducible relativism of knowledge'. And tracing the evolution of the relativist-idealist philosophy of history – from Hegel, through Nietzsche, to Croce, Gentile and beyond – White concludes that historiography culminates today in a sophisticated version of the 'Ironic condition'. The best we can do is trade in historical truth for pragmatic 'effectiveness'. A historical account is right if it *works*.[21]

In response to this radical indeterminism I would reply that the body of ascertainable evidence pertaining to a historical event deeply determines our ultimate interpretation. 'Reality must shine through', as Friedlander insists in *Probing the Limits of Representation*, 'even if indirectly'. And in reply to White's apologist plea for a 'new voice' to bear witness to past crimes, Friedlander rightly retorts that 'it is the reality and the significance of . . . catastrophies that generate the search for a new voice and not the use of a specific voice which constructs the significance of these events'.[22] We can, in short, readily accept that narrative is a world-*making* as well as a world-*disclosing* process – whose results never reach the exactitude of an algorithm or syllogism – without thereby succumbing to linguistic relativism. The fact that we acknowledge the narrative function of 'as if' in all fictional stories, and of 'as' in all histories, does not mean that we must abandon all referential claims to reality.

I would suggest, all things considered, that every narrative history be subject to *both* the external criteria of evidence *and* the internal criteria of linguistic/genre appropriateness (for example one doesn't portray Auschwitz in a tourist commercial for rural Poland). For if an appropriate balance is not struck here, it is difficult to avoid the extremes of positivism or relativism, both of which threaten the legitimacy of narrative witness. Moroever, I would insist that in addition to the *epistemological* criteria for evaluating rival accounts of history – accounts more approximate than exact – it is necessary to add *ethical* ones, that is, to serve justice as well as truth. We need to invoke as many solid criteria as possible – linguistic, scientific and moral – if we are to be able to say that one historical account is more 'real' or 'true' or 'just' than another, that one particular revision of history is more legitimate than its contrary. And we should be able to say that.

The position of extreme postmodern irony is deftly parodied by the novelist Julian Barnes in *A History of the World in 10 and a Half Chapters*. The following citations typify his subtly sardonic reasoning. 'History isn't what happened', he writes.

> History is just what historians tell us. There was a pattern, a plan, a movement, expansion, the march of democracy; it is a tapestry, a flow of events, a complex narrative, connected, explicable. One good story leads to another. First it was kings and archbishops with some offstage divine tinkering, then it was the march of ideas and the movements of masses, then little local events which mean something bigger, but all the time it's connections, progress, meaning, this led to this, this happened because of this. And we, the readers of history, the sufferers from history, we scan the pattern for hopeful conclusions, for the way ahead. And we cling to history as a series of salon pictures, conversation pieces whose

participants we can easily reimagine back into life, when all
the time it's more like a multi-media collage.

Barnes terminates his *argumentum ad absurdum* on this sobering
note:

> The history of the world? Just voices echoing in the dark;
> images that burn for a few centuries and then fade; stories,
> old stories that sometimes seem to overlap; strange links,
> impertinent connections . . . We think we know who we are,
> though we don't quite know why we are here, or how long we
> shall be forced to stay. And while we fret and writhe in
> bandaged uncertainty we fabulate. We make up a story to
> cover the facts we don't know or can't accept; we keep a few
> true facts and spin a new story round them. Our panic and our
> pain are only eased by soothing fabulation; we call it history.[23]

But fabulations are not enough. Not when it comes to the
history of individual lives nor indeed that of collective events.
Would we be happy to accept, for instance, that retelling the
horror of Auschwitz or Screbernice is a mere excercise in
fabulation? Surely not. And that is why I have been arguing
here that to admit we cannot narrate the past with *absolute
certainty* does not mean endorsing the *arbitrariness* of every
narrative. The tendency to carve an unbridgeable gulf
between empirical chronicles and fantastic stories is, I
believe, an error; for in doing so we forfeit any way of cross-
ing from one to the other. The error is, curiously, shared by
relativists and positivists (though for opposite reasons): the
relativists claim that the only criteria for interpreting the historical past are rhetorical; while the positivists hold that any
implication of narrative in the practice of historical reporting
is a distortion of the 'facts'. Both positions nonetheless deny

Narrative Matters

the links between narrative and real life, and both are, I believe, untenable.

It is oddly telling that these two arguments have been used by negationists in the death-camps controversy. While some Holocaust deniers argue that the history of the gas chambers is just 'one narrative amongst others', enforced as 'official history' by the Allies, others, including Irving and Faurisson, base their denials on the conviction that there are insufficient 'objective facts' to prove it. The latter do not see themselves as relativisitic irrationalists – as Deborah Lipstadt and others charge – but as the very opposite: uncompromising rationalists compelled to dismiss the history of the Holocaust as a 'myth' with no basis in fact![24] Far from dismissing science, these revisionists claim that the problem with Holocaust evidence is that it is not scientific enough! Such evidence cannot, they insist, be unequivocally verified as empirical history.

To counter negationism effectively, I believe that the Holocaust needs to told as both history and story. Dogmatic appeals to 'pure facts' are not sufficient when it comes to historical testimony, whether such appeals come from positivists or revisionists. The best way of respecting historical memory against revisionism is, I repeat, to combine the most effective forms of narrative witness with the most objective forms of archival, forensic and empirical evidence. For truth is not the sole prerogative of the so-called exact sciences. There is also a truth, with its corresponding understanding, that we may properly call 'narrative'. We need both.

This whole question of testimonial truth has, I would argue, been dramatically highlighted by recent tribunals on the Holocaust controversy. I believe that Judge Charles Gray was absolutely correct, for example, in his High Court ruling in London (April 2000) that David Irving was not a 'historian' but someone who 'misrepresented and distorted' historical evidence and sought to 'obliterate from memory the [depths] humanity reached'. Irving and his revisionist allies *do* seek to 'whitewash the most heinous crime in human history'. And it must be possible to state this without reservation. But not by appealing solely to some absolute scientific criterion of 'fact'. It is not because history is informed to a greater or lesser degree by storytelling that it is condemned to untruth. This is why I fully endorse here the view of the French historian Pierre Vidal-Nacquet, when he says that we can acknowledge that history is invariably mediated through narrative and *at the same time* affirm that there is something irreducible which, willy-nilly, we 'still call reality'. Without some referential claim to 'reality', however indirect, it would seem that we would have no justification at all for distinguishing between history and fiction.[25] As Julian Barnes writes, in response to his own parody of historical relativism cited above,

> We all know objective truth is not obtainable . . . but we must still believe that objective truth is obtainable; or we must believe that it is 99 per cent obtainable; or if we can't believe this we must believe that 43 per cent objective truth is better than 41 per cent. We must do so because if we don't we're lost, we fall into beguiling relativity, we value one liar's version as much as another liar's, we throw up our hands at the puzzle of it all, we admit that the victor has the right not just to the spoils but also to the truth.
>
> (p. 244)

Let me conclude by stating that what narrative promises those of us concerned with historical truth is a form of understanding which is neither absolute nor relative, but something in between. It is what Aristotle called *phronesis*, in contrast to the mere chronicling of facts or the pure abstraction of scientific *theoria*. It is closer to art than science; or, if you prefer, to a human science than to an exact one.[26] Like the architect's ruler, it is approximative but committed to lived experience. It is, perhaps, what Shakespeare was hinting at in *A Winter's Tale* when he spoke of 'an art lawful as eating'. The point is not to deny the role of storytelling in history but to recognise that its function here is different from its function in fiction. I leave the last word on the matter to Primo Levi, who speaks for those forbidden to tell their story:

> The need to tell our story to 'the rest', to make 'the rest' participate in it, had taken on for us, before our liberation and after, the character of an immediate and violent impulse, to the point of competition with our other elementary needs.[27]

In such cases, storytelling is indeed an art as lawful, and as vital, as eating.

FIVE: ETHICS (*ETHOS*)

I shall end this book with some reflections on the *ethical* role of storytelling. The most basic point to recall here is, I think, that stories make possible the ethical sharing of a common world with others in that they are invariably a mode of *discourse*. Every act of storytelling involves someone (a teller) telling something (a story) to someone (a listener) about something (a real or imaginary world).

Different approaches to narrative emphasise one or other of these roles, sometimes to the point of exclusivity. Romantic idealists and existentialists often overstress the intentional role of the 'teller', structuralists the linguistic workings of the 'story' itself, post-structuralists the receptive role of the 'reader', and materialists and realists the referential role of the 'world'. But the most judicious approach, I would argue, is that of a critical hermeneutics which holds all four coordinates of the narrative process in balance.

This allows us to recognise not only the highly complex workings of textual play, but also the referential *world of action* from which the text derives and to which it ultimately returns. The acknowledgement of a two-way passage from action to text and back again encourages us to recognise the indispensable role of human *agency*. This role is multiple, relating as it does to the agent as *author*, *actor* and *reader*. So that when we engage with a story we are simultaneously aware of a narrator (telling the story), narrated characters (acting in the story) and a narrative interpreter (receiving the story and relating it back to a life-world of action and suffering).

Without this interplay of agency I believe that we would no longer possess that sense of narrative *identity* which provides us with a particular experience of *selfhood* indispensable to any kind of moral responsibility.[28] Every moral agent must, after all, have some sense of self-identity which perdures over a lifetime of past, present and future – as well as over a communal history of predecessors, contemporaries and successors – if it is to be capable of making and keeping promises. This sense of selfhood, which MacIntyre calls the 'narrative unity of a life', ultimately derives from the question: Who are you? In other words, our life becomes an answer to the question 'who?' – usually addressed to us by another – in so far as we tell our life-story to ourselves and to others. This telling furnishes each of us with a sense of being a 'subject' capable of acting and committing ourselves to others.

Now, it is this very claim to narrative selfhood which an

overemphasising of textual indeterminacy and anonymity challenges. But the stakes are high. With the proposed obliteration of 'the experiencing, acting subject' the very idea of taking action to change the world is jeopardised.[29] And the old question: *what is to be done?* goes unanswered. Against this scenario of political paralysis I reply that storytelling is intrinsically interactive; and that apocalyptic pronouncements to the contrary, suggesting that we are assisting at the 'end of storytelling', do not consider the full consequences of their claims.

A model of narrative selfhood can, I propose, respond to anti-humanist suspicions of subjectivity while preserving a significant notion of the ethical-political subject. The best response to this crisis of self is not, I believe, to revive some foundationalist notion of the person as substance, cogito or ego. Apologetics is no answer. It is foolhardy to deny the legitimacy of many postmodern critiques of the essentialist subject. A far more appropriate strategy, I suggest, is to be found in a philosophical model of narrative which seeks to furnish an alternative model of self-identity. Namely, the narrative identity of a person, presupposed by the designation of a proper name, and sustained by the conviction that it is the same subject who perdures through its diverse acts and words between birth and death. The story told by a self about itself tells about the action of the 'who' in question: and the identity of this 'who' is a narrative one. This is what Ricoeur calls an *ipse*-self of process and promise, in contrast to a fixed *idem*-self, which responds only to the question 'what?'.[30] In sum, I would wager that no matter how cyber, digital or intergalactic our world becomes, there will always be human selves to recite and receive stories. And these narrative selves will always be capable of ethically responsible action.

The most convincing argument I have come across to date *against* the ethical character of narratives is Langer's claim that many Holocaust witnesses are split or 'diminished' selves immune to the moral criteria of 'action and evaluation'. His reasoning, touched on earlier, is that the testimonies of these survivors often bespeak shattered identities 'trying to come to terms with memories of the need to act and the simultaneous inability to do so that continue to haunt [them] today'. And because this need to act issued from an agent 'who was never in control of the consequences, the ensuing drama resists all effort at interpretation using traditional moral expectations'. We are left, he surmises, 'with a series of personal histories beyond judgment and evaluation'.[31] But the problem with Langer's refusal of a moral function to narrative memories of the Holocaust is that he risks, despite himself, condemning the survivors to the condition of a permanently 'disunited' self, which is exactly what, by his own account, the Nazis themselves tried to achieve. He thus undermines his own argument, it seems to me, when he concedes that the witness's 'diminished self' is a symptom of the 'psychological consequences of the Nazi strategy to fragment identity by allying it with disunity instead of community'.[32] To insist on seeing Holocaust testimonies in an a-moral light might then, paradoxically, be doing the Nazis' work for them. Thus while Langer duly reminds us of the limits and difficulties of narration, especially in the Holocaust context, he does not, I believe, disprove the ethical legitimacy of continuing to tell the story in spite of all. Nor, I suspect, would he want to.

Storytelling is, of course, something we participate in (as actors) as well as something we do (as agents). We are subject to narrative as well as being subjects of narrative. We are made by stories before we ever get around to making our own. Which is what makes each human existence a fabric stitched from stories heard and told. As storytellers and story-followers we are born into a certain intersubjective historicity which we inherit along with our language, ancestry and genetic code. 'We belong-to history before telling stories or writing histories. The historicity proper to story-telling and history-writing is encompassed within the reality of history.'[33] Moreover, it is because of our belonging to history as storytellers and story-followers that we are *interested* by stories – in addition to being merely *informed* by facts. History is always told with specific 'interests' in mind, as Habermas observes, the first of which is the 'interest' in communication. This interestedness is essentially ethical in that what we consider *communicable* and *memorable* is also what we consider *valuable*. What is most worthy of being preserved in memory is precisely those 'values which ruled the individual actions, the life of the institutions, and the social struggles of the past'.[34] It is with just such an interest in intersubjective sympathy in mind that Richard Rorty has recently argued for a society inspired by narrative imagination rather than doctrinal sermons or abstract treatises.

> In a moral world based on what Kundera calls the 'wisdom of the novel' moral comparisons and judgements would be made with the help of proper names rather than general terms or general principles. A society which took its moral vocabulary from novels rather than from ontico-theological or ontico-moral treatises would . . . ask itself what we can do so as to get along with each other, how we can arrange things so as to be comfortable with one another, how institutions can be changed so that everyone's right to be understood has a better chance of being gratified.[35]

Indeed, Rorty goes so far as to suggest that narratives not only help to humanise aliens, strangers and scapegoats – as Harriet Beecher Stowe's *Uncle Tom's Cabin* did, for example, regarding white prejudices against blacks – but also to make each one of us into an 'agent of love' sensitive to the particular details of others' pain and humiliation.[36]

Storytelling, we may conclude, then, is never neutral. Every narrative bears some evaluative charge regarding the events narrated and the actors featured in the narration. After all, could we truly appreciate the tragic tale of *Othello* if we were not persuaded that Iago was devious and Desdemona inno- cent? Could we really enjoy the battle between Luke Sky- walker and Darth Vader if we did not see the former as an agent of justice and the latter as a force of destruction? Or to take another tack on this question, would it make any sense to argue that *Anne Frank* is an anti-Semitic story? Or that *Oliver Twist* is an apologia for nineteenth-century capitalism? The fact that the answers are obvious is indication enough that each narra- tive carries its own weightings regarding the moral worth of its characters, and dramatises the moral relationship between certain actions and their consequences. (This is what Aristotle referred to as the emplotted relation between character, virtue and fortune in *Poetics* 1448a–1450b.) There is no narrated action that does not involve some response of approval or disapproval relative to some scale of goodness or justice – though it is always up to us readers to choose for ourselves from the various value options proposed by the narrative. The very notion of cathartic pity and fear, linked as it is to unmerited misfortune, for example, would collapse if our aesthetic responses were to be totally divorced from any empathy or antipathy towards the character's ethical quality.[37]

Far from being ethically neutral, each story seeks to

persuade us one way or another about the evaluative character of its actors and their actions. And regardless of whether we embrace these rhetorical and moral situations, we cannot pretend that they are not at work in the text's effect upon us. Stories alter our lives as we return from text to action. Every story is loaded. And while it is true to say that a story is neither good nor bad but thinking makes it so, this is so only up to a point. Granted, we deploy our own ethical presuppositions each time we respond to a story, but we always have something to respond to. The story is not confined to the mind of its author alone (the romantic fallacy regarding the primacy of the author's original intentions). Nor is it confined to the mind of its reader. Nor indeed to the action of its narrated actors. The story exists in the interplay between all these. Every story is a play of at least three persons (author/ actor/addressee) whose outcome is never final. That is why narrative is an open-ended invitation to ethical and poetic responsiveness. Storytelling invites us to become not just agents of our own lives, but narrators and readers as well. It shows us that the untold life is not worth living.

There will always be someone there to say, 'tell me a story', and someone there to respond. Were this not so, we would no longer be fully human.

THE END

Notes

ONE   WHERE DO STORIES COME FROM?

1 Hannah Arendt, *The Human Condition*, Chicago, University of Chicago Press, 1958, p. 72. See also Julia Kristeva, *Crisis of the European Subject*, New York, Other Press, 2000 and Seyla Benhabib, *Situating the Self*, New York, Routledge, 1992.

2 This volume is the first in a trilogy bearing the overall title 'Philosophy at the Limit'. The two subsequent volumes are entitled *Strangers, Gods and Monsters* (London and New York, Routledge, forthcoming 2002) and *The God who May Be* (Bloomington, IN, Indiana University Press, 2001). Each deals, in its different way, with experiences of extremity which reside at the edge of our conventional understanding, seeking to address phenomena beyond the strict frontiers of reason alone in efforts to imagine new possibilities of saying and being. The three volumes share an abiding conviction that when we are confronted with the apparently inexplicable and unthinkable, *narrative matters*.

3 See Alasdair MacIntyre, *After Virtue*, Notre Dame, Notre Dame Press, IN, 1981; Paul Ricoeur, *Time and Narrative*, 3 vols, Chicago, University of Chicago Press, 1984–8; Charles Taylor, *Sources of the Self*, Cambridge, MA, Harvard University Press, 1989; Martha Nussbaum, *Love's Knowledge: Essays on Philosophy and Literature*, Oxford, Oxford University Press, 1990.

4 See Roland Barthes, *Image, Music, Text*, London and New York, Fontana, 1977, and Fredric Jameson, *The Prisonhouse of Language*, Princeton, NJ, Princeton University Press and *The Political Unconscious: Narrative as a Socially Symbolic Act*, London, Methuen, 1981. See also the powerful critiques of the structuralist confinement of language to a self-referential system of signifiers by such thinkers as Ricoeur, *Time and*

Narrative, Chris Norris, *What is Wrong with Postmodernism?*, Baltimore, The John S. Hopkins University Press, 1990, Terry Eagleton, *The Illusion of Postmodernism*, Oxford, Blackwell, 1996, and Denis Donoghue, *Ferocious Alphabets*, Boston, MA, Little, Brown, 1981.

5 Robert Scholes and Robert Kellogg, *The Nature of Narrative*, Oxford, Oxford University Press, 1966, p. 17. J. R. R. Tolkien makes a similar point in his illuminating essay 'On Fairy-Stories', *The Tolkien Reader*, Princeton, NJ, Princeton University Press, 1968, pp. 33–90, for example when he states that 'to ask what is the origin of stories is to ask what is the origin of language and of the mind' (p. 44). He claims here that the earliest instinct for storytelling, from the very first of folk myths on, expresses an innate desire 'to hold communion with other living beings' (p. 41) – including animals, plants and even preternatural beings. So doing, stories work to create a sense of 'other' time and space where this task may be facilitated. Tolkien usefully divides the components of narrative into (1) invention, (2) inheritance and (3) the diffusive, then proceeds to isolate and discuss four central features of all great stories: *fantasy, escape, consolation* and *recovery* (pp. 47, 67f.). The fundamental motivation of all narrative art, concludes Tolkien, is to open up a 'secondary world' or 'sub-creation' which discloses truths and realities normally occluded by the primary world of ordinary perception and opinion (p. 70, also p. 89). The modern rationalist view that stories lead us into a world of illusory artifice and unreality is resisted by Tolkien, who retorts: 'A genuine fairy-story should be presented as true' (p. 42). Not that he is suggesting we collapse the two worlds – primary and secondary, lived and narrated – into one. He is quite clear that stories of the Frog-King are only possible, for example, because we can distinguish between frogs and men! Tolkien's point is subtler than the literalist or idealist monisms would allow. He is saying that precisely because it opens up an 'other' world, narrative art affords us privileged insight into the secret workings and potencies of this world.

6 Claude Lévi-Strauss, 'Shamanism and Pyschoanalysis', *Structural Anthropology*, New York, Penguin, 1968. See also S. Crites, 'The Narrative Quality of Experience', *Journal of the American Academy of Religion*, vol. 39, 1971.

7   An interesting hypothesis, offered by trauma theorists like Cathy
    Caruth in *Unclaimed Experience: Trauma, Narrative and History*, Baltimore, The
    John Hopkins University Press, 1995 and Lisa Schnell in 'Learning
    How to Tell: Narratives of Child Loss', is that one of the most prim-
    ordial functions of stories is to deal with the 'inexperienced' –
    because at the time unbearable – experience of *loss*. Schnell uses the
    Freudian model of post-traumatic stress disorder to argue that narra-
    tives, as elaborate versions of dream-work, serve to 'master the
    stimulus retrospectively, by developing the anxiety whose omission
    was the cause of the traumatic neuroses' (*Beyond the Pleasure Principle*,
    New York, Norton, 1989, p. 37). In short, when we find ourselves
    unable to deal with the traumatising shock (*Schreck*) of a certain
    accident involving inadmissible pain – such as child loss – we actu-
    ally prevent ourselves from experiencing it at the time and so need
    to retrieve the inexperienced experience after the event via narratives
    which re-present the traumatic event in a surrogate or vicarious
    fashion – thereby permitting a certain mourning anguish (*Angst*) that
    can be worked through and acknowledged. This creative repetition
    via stories releases us, Schnell argues, from the obsessional repeti-
    tion resulting from the unconscious repression of trauma. Schnell
    relates this in turn to the famous Freudian example of his grand-
    child mastering the traumatic disappearance of his mother with a
    narrative of *fort/da*: the words 'there'/'here' serving to turn the to
    and fro movement of the wooden reel into a micro-narrative – 'the
    shortest story ever', as Schnell admits, but one which still serves as a
    sort of 'creative compensation' in both word and act. When it
    comes to 'child loss' it is far less feasible, the author says, to find
    compensation through narrative, but the very attempt to put the loss
    into some kind of story, however doomed to failure, itself somehow
    contributes to the slow therapeutic healing process. In such
    instances of intolerable loss, the narrative mourner becomes like
    'Penelope with her tapestry – as long as she was still working at it,
    no-one could say that Ulysses would never come home.' Schnell
    cites Lucy Grealy in conclusion: 'sometimes, the closest we get to
    answering the saddest questions life asks us is to respond in the
    most beautiful language we can muster'. Perhaps, to use Roddy
    Doyle's phrase, stories are ways in which we endeavour to 'fill the

hole' within us, that is, survive the impossible trauma of separation, absence, death.

8   See analyses of the narrative need for storytelling in Bruno Bettelheim, *The Uses of Enchantment*, London, Penguin, 1978 and Tolkien, 'On Fairy-Stories'. One of the most basic tasks of storytelling, argues Tolkien along with Lévi-Strauss and others, is to provide narrative solutions to the conundrums of time and death. Just as Lévi-Strauss once described myths as 'machines for the suppression of time', Tolkien claims that the 'oldest and deepest desire' of all great fairy-stories is the 'Great Escape: the Escape from Death' (p. 85). *Pace* most modernist and postmodernist writers, the ancient storytellers of what Lévi-Strauss calls 'cold societies' (i.e. societies not affected by the modern Western culture of progress, speed and change) saw the 'Consolation of the Happy Ending' as a desirable narrative effect. Happy endings often included, it must be noted, some rather punitive experiences for the evil characters – for example Snow White's step-mother is forced to dance herself to death in red-hot shoes and Cinderella's sisters have their eyes pierced by doves. Curiously these bedtime-story 'horror scenes' do not appear to have disturbed children's sleep. In fact it might be argued that giving the child's inner sense of confusion, chaos, terror and evil a name and an identity, albeit imaginary, gave a sense of security and relief.

9   Tolkien, 'On Fairy-Stories', p. 65. Seamus Heaney offers a wonderful gloss on the ultimate confrontation with the dragon-figure in *Beowulf*, extending its significance to the world of adult tragic wisdom: 'Beowulf's mood as he gets ready to fight the dragon – who could be read as a projection of Beowulf's own chthonic wisdom refined in the crucible of experience – recalls the mood of other tragic heroes: Oedipus at Colonus, Lear at his "ripeness is all" extremity; Hamlet in the last illuminations of his "prophetic soul".... "He was sad at heart/ Unsettled yet ready, sensing his death/His fate hovered near, unknowable but certain" (ii. 3415–21)' (from Heaney's Introduction to his translation, *Beowulf*, New York and London, Norton, 2000, p. xx). Heaney reads the third and final part of the poem, where the ageing Beowulf fatally confronts his fate (*wyrd*) in the guise of the monstrous dragon, as the culmination of a 'work of creative imagination in which

conflicting realities find accommodation with a new order . . . and reconciliation occurs' (p. xvii). In this sense, *Beowulf* is both a tale for all times and a more localised narrative forged between the seventh and tenth centuries in response to (a) the struggles of the 'dark ages' from which the Anglo-Saxon community were then striving to emerge and (b) the more specific struggle to make sense of their complex and confused national origins – represented in the Saga by three different tribes, the Geats, Swedes and Danes. In our analysis of the narrative construction of English and British nationality in Part 3 we shall see how Ireland would come to play such a formative role *qua* 'mirror-image' in the fourteenth century and after.

10 Arundhati Roy, *The God of Small Things*, London, Flamingo, 1997, pp. 229–30. See also here Mircea Eliade, *Myths, Dreams and Mysteries*, London, Fontana, 1968.

11 Paul Ricoeur, *Time and Narrative*, trans. K. McLaughlin and D. Pellauer, Chicago: Chicago University Press, 1984–8.

TWO FROM HISTORY TO STORY: THE CASE OF STEPHEN DAEDALUS

1 One might note that the other central character of the novel, Bloom, who serves as Stephen's surrogate father and whose path he crosses for the first time in the National Library, is engaged in a similar struggle to overcome the crippling resentments of the 'cuckold bawd' (a condition of sexual betrayal which it seems Joyce suffered from no less than Shakespeare). See my more extended analysis of these themes in 'Hamlet's Ghosts – From Shakespeare to Joyce' in *Strangers, Gods and Monsters* (forthcoming 2002); and in 'Joyce: Questioning Narratives' and 'A Tale of Two Cities', *Imagining Ireland: Narratives in Modern Irish Culture*, Dublin, Wolfhound Press, 2001. On the rapport between the father–son theme and Joyce's own response to the arrival of his son Georgio, see John McCourt's excellent new biography, *The Years of Bloom: James Joyce in Trieste 1904–1920*, Dublin, Lilliput Press, 2000. If *Ulysses* is indeed one of the most innovative works of contemporary fiction, it is also a story which ingeniously transliterates Joyce's own biographical history – bearing out his avowal that 'it would be a brave man would invent something that never happened!'. That is the paradox of all great fiction.

2 Maurice Blanchot, *The Writing of Disaster*, Lincoln, NB, University of Nebraska Press, 1986 and commentary by Lawrence Langer in *Holocaust Testimonies*, New Haven and London, Yale University Press, 1991, pp. 69, 132, 158–60. See also the suggestive readings of both Blanchot and Beckett by Simon Critchley, *Very Little . . . Almost Nothing: Death, Philosophy and Literature*, London and New York, Routledge, 1997. For a contrasting view of narrative as expanding and amplifying our powers of vision – closer to Joyce than Beckett – see Milan Kundera, *The Art of the Novel*, New York, Grove Press, 1988 and Martha Nussbaum's insightful analysis of the role literary imagination plays in the development of ethical self-knowledge and judgement in *Love's Knowledge*, Oxford, Oxford University Press, 1990, especially the following studies: 'Flawed Crystals: James's The Golden Bowl and Literature as Moral Philosophy', 'Finely Aware and Richly Responsible: Literature and the Moral Imagination', 'Perceptive Equilibrium: Literary Theory and Ethical Theory', 'Reading for Life', 'Fictions of the Soul' and 'Narrative Emotions'. Several of Nussbaum's arguments for an ethical narrative imagination find support in other contemporary theories – for example Arthur Danto's idea of 'transfigurative literature', Northrop Frye's notion of 'educated imagination', Frank Lentriccia's concept of 'art for life's sake', Wayne Booth's plea for an 'ethics of reading' and Iris Murdoch's claim that 'art is the most educational thing we have'.

3 See my exploration of the post-Joycean movements in Irish fiction in 'A Crisis of Fiction' in *Imagining Ireland*. On the role of fiction in the narrative reconstruction of history, see the intriguing remark of Irish novelist and film-maker Neil Jordan: 'Treat history as fiction in the making: a fiction that will create a future'. See Luke Gibbons, 'Demisting the Screen', *Irish Literary Supplement*, Spring 1997, pp. 16–18.

4 Roddy Doyle, *A Star Called Henry*, New York: Viking, 1999, p. 7.

5 Dermot Healy, *The Bend for Home*, London, Harvill Press, 1996, p. 57.

6 Tolkien, 'On Fairy-Stories', p. 88.

7 Healy, *The Bend for Home*, pp. 59–60.

8 Robert McLiam Wilson, *Eureka Street*, London, Martin Secker and Warburg, 1996, p. 22. See also 215–16. Other young Irish writers to explore the relationship between fiction and history include Ronan Sheehan, Neil Jordan and James Ryan.

THREE WHOSE STORY IS IT ANYWAY? THE CASE OF DORA

1 See S. Freud, *The Standard Edition of the Complete Psychological Works*, London, Hogarth Press, 1953–74, vol. 5.

2 Adam Phillips, 'The Telling of Selves', *On Flirtation*, London, Faber, 1994, p. 73.

3 Elaine Showalter, *Hystories: Hysterical Epidemics and Modern Media*, New York, Columbia University Press, 1997, pp. 42–3.

4 J. Masson, *Against Therapy*, London, Fontana, 1990, p. 101 and also his more general attack on the psychoanalytic exploitation of memory in *The Assault on Truth: Freud's Suppression of the Seduction Theory*, New York, Farrar Strauss Giroux, 1984.

5 See also the useful review article by Marjorie Orr, 'Recovered Memory', *Addiction Today*, Jan.–Feb. 1999, pp. 17–20. Orr begins with a quote from Dori Laub's *Testimony*, 1992: 'The not telling of the story serves as a perpetration of its tyranny. . . . When one's history is abolished one's identity ceases to exist as well.' She then goes on to cite studies which show that recovered memories are just as accurate as continuous memories of abuse, in spite of the almost total media denial of traumatic amnesia. Of the 'dissociative-identity-disorder patients who recovered repressed abuse memories, 68% were able to find outside corroboration. One of the easiest forms of retrieved memories after traumatic amnesia to receive external confirmation were those documented by the two World Wars, the Middle East war and Vietnam. For example Hugh Thompson, an American pilot honoured by Bill Clinton for his part in stopping the My Lai massacre, suffered severe post-traumatic stress disorder and dissociation and actually remembered nothing when interviewed two years later.'

6 As Walter Reich argues in his essay 'The Monster in the Mist: Are Long Buried Memories of Child Abuse Reliable?' (a critical review essay of books by M. Yapko, L. Terr and L. Wright in *The New York Times Review of Books*, 15 May 1994). See also Elaine Showalter on the recovered memory syndrome, especially in relation to the Ingram case, in *Hystories*, pp. 154, 186f. I have dealt with some of these issues separately in 'Narrative and the Ethics of Remembrance' in *Questioning Ethics*, ed. R. Kearney and M. Dooley, London and New York, Routledge, 1998.

7 See Stephen Marcus, 'Freud and Dora: Story, History, Case History'

and Jane Gallop, 'Keys to Dora', in *Dora's Case*, ed. Claire Kahane and C. Bernheimer, New York, University of Columbia Press, 1990.

8   Robert Coles, *The Call of Stories*, Boston, Houghton Mifflin Company, 1989, p. 7.

9   Ibid., pp. 22–3. For Lévi-Strauss's distinction between the scientist and shaman see 'Psychoanalysis and Shamanism', *Structural Anthropology*, New York, Penguin, 1963. Sometimes the role of shaman can be taken to extremes, as in the case of certain therapy gurus who take on the role of saviour-hero for their clients. Even Jung was not immune to such *salvator* fantasies, as is evident from biographical accounts of his therapeutic relationship with his lover-analysand Toni, in which he acted out the hero role of certain ancient myths.

10   Frank Cioffi, 'Wittgenstein's Freud', pp. 11–12, cited in *The Memory Wars: Freud's Legacy in Dispute*, ed. Frederick Crews et al., London, Granta, 1995.

11   Crews, *The Memory Wars*, pp. 12–13.

12   Adam Phillips, *On Flirtation*, London, Faber, 1994, pp. 86 and 144. See also Malcolm Bowie, *Psychoanalysis and the Future of Theory*, Oxford, Blackwell, 1993 and Christopher Bollas, *Being a Character: Psychoanalysis*, New York, Hill and Wang, 1992.

13   See R. Schafer, *Retelling a Life: Narration and Dialogue in Psychoanalysis*, New York, Basic Books, 1992 and *Narrative Actions in Psychoanalysis*, Worcester, MA, Clark University Press, 1981. I am indebted to Charles Guignon for bringing these arguments to my attention, especially in his article 'Narrative Explanation in Psychotherapy', *American Behavioural Scientist*, vol. 41, no. 4, January 1998, pp. 558–75. Guignon makes the point that both the scientist (naturalist/postivist/behaviourist) approach and the constructivist (idealist/psychologist/subjectivist) approach presuppose the same old split between subject and object. The only difference between the two, he argues, is that where constructionists 'invite us to celebrate the fact that the meanings we create swing free of any ties to reality, naturalists encourage us to expunge all meaning vocabulary from our theories so that we can be sure we are getting in touch with reality as it is in itself' (p. 567). Guignon himself espouses a more 'hermeneutic' narrativist approach, similar to my own – though owing more to Heidegger and Gadamer than Ricoeur and Kristeva – which argues that the events of the past become significant in the

context of a narrative which rereads them in the light of our projection of where 'the story is going as a whole' (p. 574). I am also grateful to the useful insights on this question provided by my former doctoral student James Sheehan, in 'Liberating Narrational Styles in Systemic Practice', *Journal of Systemic Therapies*, vol. 18, no. 3, 1999, pp. 51–67, and 'Psychotherapy as Narrative: A Critical Application of Paul Ricoeur's Philosophy of Narrative to Psychotherapy', Ph.D. thesis at University College Dublin, 1995. See also here the helpful discussions of the hermeneutic approach to narrative in *On Paul Ricoeur: Narrative and Interpretation*, ed. David Wood, London and New York, Routledge, 1991 (in particular the essays by D. Wood, J. Ree, J. Bernstein and H. White); and in *Paul Ricoeur: The Hermeneutics of Action*, ed. R. Kearney, London, Sage, 1996 (especially the essays by D. Rasmussen, J. Dunne, P. Kemp, D. Jervolino and J. Greisch). See, finally, Ciarán Benson's insightful exploration of the narrative structures of the self drawing from the more psychological approach of Jerry Brunner and Rom Harré in *The Cultural Psychology of the Self*, London, Routledge, 2001.

14 Cited and commented by Adam Phillips, *On Flirtation*, p. 66.
15 Ibid., p. 73. Even personal diaries and journals, it could be said, are implicitly addressed to another, even if it is an alter-ego of the diarist her/himself as s/he imagines her/himself to be, residing at some remove from the immediacy of the experiences described in the diary itself.
16 As J. B. Pontalis said, 'One shouldn't write one autobiography but ten of them, or a hundred because, while we have only one life we have innumerable ways of recounting that life to ourselves.' And as another analyst, Adam Phillips, adds, it takes even more numerous ways to retell our lives to other people! Which is why every story is a betrayal – in the double sense of both revealing the past and traducing it by turning it into something in the present act of speech which is of necessity partially different from what it was in the past, that is, supposing we could ever have direct access to the past precisely as past. See Phillips's insightful commentary on this complex process of recounting life-stories, wavering between what I would call an anti-narrativist and neo-narrativist stance (pp. 68–9). See here Ricoeur's accounts of this task of renarrating the paralysed past in 'Memory and Forgetting', in *Questioning Ethics*, ed. M. Dooley and R. Kearney, London and New

York, Routledge, 1999 and *La Mémoire, L'histoire, L'oubli*, Paris, Le Seuil, 2000. In the light of the above analysis of the various narratives offered by Dora and Freud and later by his many critics and disciples, I am compelled to concede that my own reading is yet another narrative attempt – among many – to make some sense of 'Dora's Story'. In short, philosophical accounts themselves constitute narratives of what we might call a 'third level' kind, though their authors frequently wish to deny this in the interests of so-called 'scientific objectivity'.

FOUR TESTIFYING TO HISTORY: THE CASE OF SCHINDLER

1 See the illuminating discussions of the German *Historikerstreit* in Saul Friedlander (ed.), *Probing the Limits of Representation: Nazism and the 'Final Solution'*, Cambridge, MA, Harvard University Press, 1992, especially Dominick LaCapra, 'Representing the Holocaust: Reflections on the Historians' Debate', pp. 108–28.

2 See Paul Ricoeur, 'The Memory of Suffering', *Figuring the Sacred: Religion, Narrative and Imagination*, Minneapolis, Fortress Press, 1995, p. 290.

3 Cited by Stephen Feinstein, *Witness and Legacy: Contemporary Art about the Holocaust*, Center for Holocaust and Genocide Studies, University of Minnesota, Minneapolis, Lerner Publications Company, 2000, p. 8f. See also the useful documents on the subject of representing and remembering historical genocides and other atrocities in the publication accompanying the *Face à l'histoire* exhibition, Centre Georges Pompidou, Paris, April 1997; and the publication, CD Rom and experimental art exhibit entitled *Immemory* (1998) accompanying Chris Marker's *Level Five*, a filmic exploration of the problem of recording historical massacres and catastrophes (for example Okinawa) through images.

4 Feinstein, *Witness and Legacy*, p. 10. See Stephen Feinstein's persuasive defence of *Maus*, ibid., p. 18:

> As Spiegelman progressed into the drawing of Maus, he became concerned with various aesthetic aspects that were important from the point of view of the visual artist. He was becoming increasingly concerned with deconstructing the basic narrative and visual elements of the comic strip: How does one panel on a page relate to others? How

do a strip's artificial cropping and use of pictorial illusion manipulate
reality? . . . How do words and pictures combine in the human brain?
In this quest, the artist rejected photo-realism, elaborate detailing and
shading, and ultimately developed a particular reduction process in
which text was reduced to fit the artistic space.

5   Elie Wiesel, *One Generation After*, New York, Avon Books, 1970, p. 15.
In 'In Art and Culture After the Holocaust' (in *Auschwitz: Beginning of a
New Era?*, ed. Eva Fleischner, KTAV Publishing House, USA, 1974),
Wiesel appears even more disillusioned with the role of narrative
testimony:

> After the war, every survivor was asked the same question by the dead:
> Will you be able to tell *our* tale? Now we know the answer: no. Their tale
> cannot be told – and never will be. Those who spoke were not heard;
> the story you heard was not the story they told.
>
> (p. 404)

Terrence Des Pres makes a similar observation to Wiesel's in *The
Survivor*: 'Insofar as we feel compelled to defend a comforting view of
life, we tend to deny the survivor's voice' (*The Survivor: An Anatomy of Life
in the Death Camps*, New York, Pocket Books, 1976, pp. 3–34). And yet in
spite of such candid reservations, Des Pres, like Wiesel, insists on the
necessity to go on testifying *on behalf of the otherwise forgotten dead*:

> Whoever comes through will take with him the burden of speaking for
> the others. Someone will survive and death will not be absolute. This
> small pledge, this gigantic demand, is intensely important to people
> facing extinction. . . . In the survivor's voice the dead's own scream is
> active.
>
> (pp. 38–40)

A similar sense of moral duty to record the scream of the dead is
evident in *Alicia* by Alicia Appleman-Jurman, New York, Bantam,
1988. I am grateful to my graduate student Robert Erlewine for
bringing many of these sources to my attention.
6   Feinstein, *Witness and Legacy*, p. 19.
7   See Gabriel Schoenfeld, 'Death Camps as Kitsch', *The New York Times*,
18 March 1999. See also Judith Miller (*One, By One, By One: Facing the
Holocaust*, New York, Simon and Schuster, 1990):

This vulgarisation is a new form of historical titillation. And in a society like America's, where the public attention span is measured in seconds and minutes rather than years or decades, where fad is often confused with trend, where sentimentality replaces insight, it represents a considerable threat to dignified remembrance.

(p. 232)

Karl Plank called this voyeuristic approach to the Holocaust the 'hermeneutic of Cain', which he contrasts with the genuine hermeneutic of the witness. Only the latter, he argues, tries to testify from the inside, though even here we must be wary of facile or overhasty identifications. 'What happened THERE is unlike what happened HERE and cannot be reduced to or explained by its categories' (The Mother of the Wire Fence: Inside and Outside the Holocaust, Louisville, Westminster John Knox Press, 1994, p. 45). One of the most controversial novelistic retellings of the Holocaust accused of voyeuristic opportunism and exploitation is D. M. Thomas's The White Hotel, New York, Viking, 1981. See the informative article by Mary-Jo Hughes, 'Revelations in The White Hotel', in Critique, Fall 1985, pp. 37–50.

8   Lanzmann, 'Holocaust: la représentation impossible', Le Monde, February 1994.

9   J.-F. Lyotard, Heidegger and the 'Jews', Minneapolis, Minnesota University Press, 1988.

10   Lawrence Langer, Holocaust Testimonies, New Haven, Yale University Press, 1991, p. 97. See also pp. 129, 138, 148–9, 157–61, 171–5, 182–3, 188–9, 192–3.

11   Shoshana Felman and Dori Laub, Testimony, New York, Routledge, 1992, pp. 218–19. Lawrence Langer makes a strong argument in favour of oral versus written, filmed or reconstructed testimony in Holocaust Testimonies. His basic point is that all narrative retelling risks altering what is being told. The difference between written memoirs like those of Charlotte Delbo, Primo Levi, Jean Amery or Elie Wiesel and the direct oral witness of taped or recorded survivors is that the latter includes silences and gestures that cannot be duplicated on the written page (or screenplay) and 'above all a freedom from the legacy of literary form and precedent to which anyone attempting a written narrative on any subject is indebted' – for example chronology, plot,

description, dialogue, moral evaluation, point-of-view, retrospective editorial selection, or the invention of a narrative voice. Such a narrative voice above all, according to Langer, distorts the reality of the recalled event, for it seeks to 'impose on apparently chaotic episodes a perceived sequence, whether or not that sequence was perceived in an identical way during the period that is being rescued from oblivion by memory and language' (p. 41). Langer's point is basically that the most honest form of witness may be the recognition of the failure and futility of narrative memory – the exposure of an absolute rupture between the dead past and living present which no amount of synthesising-schematising-emplotting can turn into some kind of narrative coherence or connection. In short, genuine oral testimony is experienced as cessation rather than as continuity, marking an inaccessibly absent or 'dead time' that cannot be resurrected or retrieved by storytelling. The most authentic witness is what Langer calls the 'impromptu self' whose fragmented oral testimony expresses the irretrievable breakdown of narrative time and history (pp. 129, 138, 148–9, 157–61, 171–5, 182–3, 188–9, 192–3). In reply to Langer I would be inclined to say that even the most extreme form of what he calls 'anguished' or 'humiliated' memories, where the witnesses express deep anxiety about the lack of common ground between the reality they suffered and the words they are now trying to use (pp. 64, 83, 97), is still a form of narrative memory, albeit radically altered. For we are only able to experience the very futility and failure of survivors' narratives because they are trying, however impossibly, to narrate the unnarratable. This I would not call 'non-story', with Langer and Blanchot, but rather 'impossible story' – which, however truncated, disjunctive or deconstructed it may be, is still a story. A story in ruins, granted, but a story nonetheless. In short, not every story has to involve processes of integration, harmony and compensation. That is only a limited definition of narrative as 'happy ending' consolation, associated with certain conservative conventions of classic realist novels or folktales. The testimonial narratives of the Holocaust are, needless to say, of an entirely different order; but they do not, I would insist, represent the abandonment of narrative tout court. What would we know of the crime of the Belzec Camp, for example, if the 2 survivors of the

600,000 inmates had not tried to tell their story, however impossible it was for them to do so?

12 Felman and Laub, *Testimony*, p. 219.

13 Ibid., p. 224. See here Hannah Arendt's own paradoxical attitude to this question of testimony. On the one hand, we have her very pessimistic view in *The Origins of Totalitarianism* that the 'radical evil' of Nazism manufactured appealing 'holes of oblivion' in which any kind of moral witness or martyrdom was impossible. On the other hand, in her later book, *Eichmann in Jerusalem*, she insists that there will always be someone to survive the terror and tell the story, concluding that 'the holes of oblivion do not exist'. For a sensitive discussion of this issue see Claudia Roth Pierpont, 'Hearts and Minds', *Passionate Minds*, New York, Vintage, 2000, pp. 255–6, 280–1.

14 See also L. Langer on the impossibility of memory in *Holocaust Testimonies*, pp. 119–20, 158–60. Writing of this double injunction – you can't believe it/you must believe it – in Srebnik's testimony, Saul Friedlander usefully underlines the importance of a certain 'narrative margin' sustained by distancing devices: 'Reality was there, in its starkness, but perceived through a filter: that of memory (distance in time), that of spatial displacement, that of some sort of narrative margin which leaves the unsayable unsaid' (S. Friedlander, *Probing the Limits of Representation*, Cambridge, MA, Harvard University Press, 1992, p. 17f.). This is a very pertinent comment. A similar 'narrative margin' is, I would suggest, successfully operative in Arnaud des Pallières's film *Drancy Avenir* (1997).

FIVE   THE PARADOX OF TESTIMONY

1 Ricoeur, *Time and Narrative*, vol. 3, p. 188. See also here Adam Phillips, 'Depression', *On Flirtation*, pp. 86–7. Here Phillips cites Bettelheim's curious point that those who best survived in the death camps were the ones best able to go mute, numb, blocking their ability to feel, represent or imagine in the face of such horror. But he adds in response: 'But if it is our destructiveness that makes us speechless, the risk is that our speechlessness makes us more destructive, and particularly of ourselves' (p. 87). A similar scruple is expressed by Celan's oblique poetic testimonies to the Shoah whose very idiosyncrasies and

opacities defy the tendency to reify or banalise the event but risk at times, it could be said, losing their readership.

2 Miller, *One, By One, By One*, p. 287.

3 Ricoeur, *Time and Narrative*, vol. 3, p. 186.

4 Szymon Laks, *Music of Another World*, Evanston, Northwestern University Press, 1999, p. 5.

5 Ibid.

6 Langer, *Holocaust Testimonies*, pp. 110f.

7 Ibid.

8 Ibid., pp. 119–20f., 173.

9 Ibid., pp. 157–61. Langer himself comes close to proposing some response to this dilemma when he makes the following distinction between the conjunctive function of story and the disjunctive function of plot, pp. 174–5:

> Ordinarily, we would expect the process of remembering, through a recovery of images and episodes, to animate the past. But former victims who reencounter Holocaust reality through testimony often discover . . . a disjunction between 'consciously remembering', in order to reveal to us what they already know, and the sense of 'being possessed' by moments or events that have never left them. This forces us to alter our traditional notion of testimony, which presumes a chronology or sequence and the act of retreating in time and space to a period and place preceding and different from the present.

Langer goes on to explain:

> Two clocks dominate the landscape of Holocaust testimonies, a time clock (ticking from then to now) and a space clock (ticking from here to here). They seek to sensitize our imaginations to twin currents of remembered experience. One flows uninterruptedly from . . . past to present. The other meanders, coils back on itself, contains rocks and rapids and requires strenuous effort to follow its intricate turns, turns that impede the mind's instinctive tropism toward tranquillity.

In literary terms, this translates into a tension between the chrono-logical story, running from 'I was captured' to 'I was liberated', and the plot which exposes the witness 'seized' by incidents and details embedded in trauma and resistant to normal temporality. The very notion of 'arrival in Auschwitz' is both a temporal-historical and a psychological-achronic event, 'tellable and told as story *and* plot'. Or as Langer puts it, while the *story* allows us to 'pass through and beyond the place', the *plot* by contrast

> stops the chronological clock and fixes the moment permanently in memory . . . immune to the vicissitudes of time. The unfolding story brings relief, while the unfolding plot induces pain. Like the witness, we struggle to synchronise the two: the most precarious challenges arise when this proves to be impossible.

10   Helen Bamber, *The Good Listener*, London, Weidenfeld and Nicolson, 1998, pp. 88–9.
11   Ibid.
12   Ibid., p. 105
13   Cited in Friedlander, *Probing the Limits of Representation*, p. 3.
14   Ibid., pp. 5–6, 96, 177, 207, 277, 320–5.
15   Ricoeur, 'The Memory of Suffering', p. 290:

> We must remember because remembering is a *moral duty*. We owe a *debt* to the victims. And the tiniest way of paying our debt is to tell and retell what happened at Auschwitz. . . . By remembering and telling, we not only prevent forgetfulness from killing the victims twice; we also prevent their life stories from becoming banal . . . and the events from appearing as necessary.

SIX   INTRODUCTION

1   Julia Kristeva, 'Strangers to Ourselves: The Hope of the Singular', in Richard Kearney (ed.), *States of Mind: Dialogues with Contemporary Thinkers*, New York, New York University Press, 1995, p. 9. Later in the same dialogue, Kristeva argues that

> we have to take seriously the violence of identity desires. For instance when somebody recognises him or herself in an X or Y origin, it can appear very laudable, a very appealing need for identity. But one mustn't forget the violence behind this desire . . . giving rise to fratricidal wars. So we need to recognise not only the relativeness of human fraternity but the need, both pedagogical and therapeutic, to take account of the death wish, of the violence *within us*.
>
> (p. 12)

2   Thomas Mann, *Joseph and his Brothers*, 4 vols, trans. H. Lowe-Porter, New York, Knopf, 1948, pp. 1026–8. This basic religious need to tell and retell the founding stories of Genesis etc. runs from the Bible itself, which contains both Hebraic and Christian retellings of the originating typological narratives so deftly analysed by Northrop Frye in *The Great Code*, to a whole subsequent history of theological and literary retellings passing through Milton and Thomas Mann down to the latest cyber version, *Neon Genesis Evangelion: The Gospel of the New Century*, an extraordinarily popular video series with millions of viewers around the world. J. R. R. Tolkien suggests that the reason such stories of a coming Kingdom endure throughout the ages is that they express a deep archetypal *evangelion* of Creation of which each narrative retelling is in some sense a sub-creation. More specifically, he claims that the Scriptures

> contain a fairy-story, or a story of a larger kind which embraces all the essence of fairy-stories. They contain many marvels – peculiarly artistic, beautiful, and moving: 'mythical' in their perfect, self-contained significance. . . . But this story has entered History and the primary world; the desire and aspiration of sub-creation has been raised to the fulfilment of Creation. . . . This story begins and ends in joy. It has pre-eminently the 'inner consistency of reality'. There is no tale ever told that men would rather find was true, and none which so many sceptical men have accepted as true on its own merits. For the Art of it has the supremely convincing tone of Primary Art, that is, of Creation. . . . God is the Lord, of angels, and of men – and of elves. Legend and History have met and fused.

The hope of every believing storyteller is, Tolkien concludes, that in 'Fantasy he may actually assist in the effoliation and multiple enrichment of creation'. In short, all great stories prefigure the Great Story. See 'On Fairy-Stories', pp. 88–9. Many depth psychologists from Jung and Von Franz to Campbell and Eliade would make similar points, except for them the fundamental narratives would be less specifically biblical and Christian than archetypal expressions of a collective unconscious revealed through the comparative analysis of mythologies, anthropologies, theologies and literatures from antiquity to modernity.

3   See Ricoeur, 'Memory–Forgetfulness–History', ZIF, vol. 2, Universität

Bielefeld, 1995, pp. 12–13. See also Ricoeur's discussion of 'la mémoire empêchée' and the healing role of pardon and amnesty etc. in *La Mémoire, L'histoire, L'oubli*.

SEVEN ROMAN FOUNDATION MYTHS: AENEAS AND ROMULUS

1 H. White, *Metahistory*, Baltimore and London, The Johns Hopkins University Press, p. 5.

2 Pascale Quignard, *Le Sexe et l'effroi*, Paris, Gallimard, 1994, pp. 24–30, 325–6, 355.

3 Eliade, *Myths, Dreams and Mysteries*, London, Fontana, 1968. See also my application of this reading to Irish political and literary narratives in 'Myth and Motherland', *Postnationalist Ireland*, London and New York, Routledge, 1997, pp. 188–121, and 'Myth and Martyrdom', *Imagining Ireland*.

4 See C. Lévi-Strauss, *Tristes Tropiques*, Harmondsworth, Penguin, 1992 and J.-F. Lyotard, *The Postmodern Condition*, Manchester, Manchester University Press, 1984.

5 Homi Bhaba, 'DissemiNation: Time, Narrative and the Margins of the Modern Nation', in *Nation and Narration*, ed. H. Bhabha, London, Routledge, 1990.

6 S. Freud, *On the Interpretation of Dreams*, New York, Penguin, 1976.

EIGHT BRITAIN AND IRELAND: A TALE OF SIAMESE TWINS

1 It is of course true that the Irish nation had some primitive sense of itself before this reaction to the fourteenth-century plantation. It has been argued, by Proinsias McCana, for example, that some form of centralised unitary government began to emerge as early as the ninth century in response to the Viking invasions, and again in the twelfth century in response to the Anglo-Norman invasion. But these intermittent efforts at all-island structures of self-rule were largely a matter of self-defence rather than any self-conscious asser-tion of enduring national identity. After all, the term 'scotus' could as easily refer to an inhabitant of Ireland as of Britain up to the eleventh century (for example John Scotus Eriugena from the for-mer, Duns Scotus from the latter). See, for example, Proinsias

McCana, 'The Early Irish Concept of Unity', *The Crane Bag*, vol. 2, nos 1 and 2, Dublin, 1978.

2 See Perry Curtis, *Apes and Angels*, New York, The Smithsonian Institution Press, 1971, and for the Kingsley and other related quotations see G. Watson, *Irish Identity and the Irish Literary Revival*, London, Croom Helm, 1979. One finds a most subtle analysis of the whole dialectic of Irish and British stereotypes in Declan Kiberd's *Inventing Ireland*, London, Vintage, 1996. One might also mention here the critical controversies surrounding the representation of Irish historical events such as the 1840s Famine (for example Kevin Whelan, *The Killing Snows: The Famine in History and Memory*, Cork, Cork University Press, 2001), the 1916 Dublin Rising and the subsequent Anglo-Irish War of Independence in contemporary Irish cinema (Luke Gibbons, 'Demisting the Screen', *Irish Literary Supplement*, Spring 1997, pp. 16–18. Gibbons discusses here the resolution by Neil Jordan, director of the major Irish bio-epic *Michael Collins*, to 'treat history as fiction in the making: a fiction that will create the future'.)

3 See Seamus Heaney, *Beowulf*, New York and London, Norton, 2000. Heaney writes interestingly of the existence of monsters outside and inside the national refuge of warrior rank and ceremony. The poem, he observes, contains

> no very clear map-sense of the world, more an apprehension of menaced borders, of danger gathering beyond the mere and the marshes, of *mearc-stapas* 'prowling the moors, huge marauders/and from other worlds'. Within these phantasmal boundaries, each Lord's hall is an actual and symbolic refuge.
>
> (p. xv)

By contrast, the dragon who faces Beowulf in the final sequence is a monster from within:

> The dragon is a given of his home ground (unlike Grendel and mother who enter from outside) abiding in his *underearth* as in his understanding, waiting for the meeting, the watcher at the ford, the questioner who sits so sly . . . against whom Beowulf's body and soul must measure themselves. Dragon equals shadow-line, the Psalmist's valley of the shadow of death, the embodiment of a knowledge deeply ingrained in the species.
>
> (p. xix)

4 See here the pioneering research of new feminist scholars such as Gerardine Meaney, 'Penelope, or Myths Unravelling' (*Textual Practice*, vol. 14, no. 3, 2000, pp. 519–29), and Margaret Kelleher, 'Irish Famine in Literature', in *The Great Irish Famine*, ed. C. Poirteir, Cork, Mercier Press, 1995, pp. 232–48.

5 As R. R. Davies points out in his landmark study 'The Peoples of Britain and Ireland 1100–1400' (*Transactions of the Royal Historical Society*, London, Royal Historical Society, 1994), the settlers in Ireland were so unsure of their own ambiguous status as a 'middle nation' – neither fully English nor fully Irish – that they demonised the native Irish as their 'other' in order to insist more emphatically on their belonging to England. A scapegoating campaign against the indigenous population followed, bolstered up with accompanying statutes and racist rhetoric, thus preventing the match between people and polity which was achieved in England by the fifteenth century from occurring in Ireland. On this role of historical distortion and amnesia in the formation of national communities and the consequent need for critical reinterpretation and remembering, see Mark Dooley, 'The Catastrophe of Memory', in *Questioning God: Religion and Postmodernism*, ed. J. Caputo, M. Scanlon and M. Dooley, Bloomington, IN, Indiana University Press, 2001. Dooley endorses Derrida's claim that deconstruction is an attempt to initiate 'a movement towards the liberation of memory', by emancipating 'spectres and ghosts' from their forgotten past so that they may come again (*revenir*) in the future. See also here J. Derrida, 'The Force of Law: "The Mystical Foundation of Authority"', in *Deconstruction and the Possibility of Justice*, ed. D. Cornell et al., New York, Routledge, 1992.

6 Linda Colley, *Forging the Nation, 1797–1837*, New Haven, Yale University Press, 1992.

7 Linda Colley, 'Britishness and Irishness', *Journal of British Studies*, no. 31, 1992, p. 72. Colley also has a deft analysis of France as Britain's traditional 'other' to the immediate south. Like Ireland to the immediate west, France was considered subversively rebellious, Catholic and 'impure'. And again like Ireland, France was once part of the original Imperial Kingdom. After all, England and France were virtually an identical kingdom from the Anglo-Norman invasion in the twelfth century up to the fifteenth century (the burning of Joan of Arc). It is easy to forget that the legendary English King Richard the Lion-Heart

– of Robin Hood and Crusader fame – was actually a French-speaker called 'Richard Coeur-de-Lion'!

8 Where Ireland had the advantage over England/Britain, then as now, is that it never achieved indivisible sovereignty as a unitary nation – and so never could mistake the illusion for a reality. For the Irish, from ancient legend to the present day, the idea of sovereignty was linked to the story of a 'fifth province': a place of mind rather than of territory, a symbol rather than a *fait accompli* (the Irish for province is *coicead*, meaning a fifth, but there are only four provinces in Ireland). See my chapters 'The Fifth Province' in *Postnationalist Ireland*, London, Routledge, 1997, pp. 99–107, and 'Towards a Postnationalist Archipelago', *The Edinburgh Review*, no. 103, 2000, reprinted in *Imagining Ireland*.

9 One should not underestimate, however, the power of residual nationalist backlashes. Note, for example, the intervention of Tory MP Gerald Howarth, a member of the Commons Home Affairs Select Committee, who opposed a recent call for a post-national Britain, arguing that the great British nation was overwhelmingly homogenous, white and Anglo-Saxon. 'We should not engage in flagellation over our glorious past', he declared. 'I for one am proud of our imperial heritage' (BBC News, 11 October 2000). Sinister echoes here of Oswald Mosley's famous invocation of the term 'alien' to scaremonger the British public in the 1930s, greeted by the infamous headline in the popular *Daily Mail*, 'Hurray for the Blackshirts' (January 1936).

NINE   AMERICA AND ITS 'OTHERS': FRONTIER STORIES

1 I discuss this dialectic of 'otherness' in the constitution of British, Irish and European identities in my *Postnationalist Ireland* (London, Routledge, 1996). See also the theological relation between sacrificial scapegoating, legitimation narratives and national identity analysed by Regina Schwartz, *The Curse of Cain: The Violent Legacy of Monotheism*, Chicago, Chicago University Press, 1997. On the role of the them-versus-us ideology of German nationalism see also Jürgen Habermas, 'Struggles for Recognition in the Democratic Constitutional State', in *Multiculturalism*, ed. Amy Gutman, Princeton, Princeton University Press, 1994, pp. 138–40, 143–6.

2 See Michel Foucault's analysis of the ship of fools in *Madness and Civilisation* (London, Random House, 1965) and my own commentary in

Modern Movements in European Philosophy (Manchester and New York, Manchester University Press, 1994), p. 292f.

3   Norman Cohn offers a fascinating account of the foundational logic of scapegoating and witchhunting in *The Pursuit of the Millennium* (London, Secker and Warburg, 1957). See also J. Ellul, *Propaganda: The Formation of Men's Attitudes*, New York, Vintage, 1973.

4   F. Bordewich, *Killing the White Man's Indian*, New York, Anchor, 1997. The repressed ghost of the 'Native-American' Stranger is making its voice heard again as more and more Native-American tribes invoke the US Constitution to reclaim sovereignty over their reservations. See Alan Wolfe's more sanguine view of American identity in *One Nation after All* (New York, Viking, 1998). The one exception to American tolerance is, the author somewhat blithely notes, homosexuality – an interesting candidate for the alien-as-insider phobia. Americans have a single national identity, concludes Wolfe, in that they are all bound together by common values of 'nonjudgmentalism' and 'capacious individualism'. See also the useful critical discussion of the relationship between recollected 'national narratives' and defendants' legal rights in Mark Osiel, *Mass Atrocity, Collective Memory, and the Law*, Somerset, NJ, Transaction Publishers, 1997, especially pp. 59–79.

5   'The Death of Slavery', *God's Stone in the Pool of Slavery*, p. 334. See also W. Jordan, *White Over Black: American Attitudes toward the Negro, 1550–1812*, New York, Norton, 1977.

6   The alien phobia first emerged as a national obsession in response to post-Second World War feelings of apocalypse, disillusionment and menace. What could still be considered fun at the time of Orson Welles's famous broadcast-hoax about aliens landing in New York began to take on more sinister and sombre tones from the 1950s and 1960s onwards. The sense of suspicion and hysteria generated, for example, by the alleged Roswell capture of alien specimens (see the *Autopsy of an Alien* documentary), in the context of a general Cold War fear of 'external enemies' and 'spies', was taking its toll. This growing paranoia was itself reflected in the rise of popular TV shows such as *The Twilight Zone* in the 1960s (see in particular the episode 'The Monsters are Due on Maple Street', first aired on 3 April 1960 with the telling warning that 'the tools of conquest do not necessarily come with bombs. . . . There are weapons that are simply thoughts'); or again the

equally popular television series *V*, aired between 1983 and 1985, which featured aliens as seemingly innocuous creatures who are secretly cold-blooded reptilians who eat rats and are bent on the silent destruction of America from within. I am indebted to my graduate students, in particular Brian Peltonen, Matt Pelletier and John Manoussakis, for several of these references.

TEN CONCLUSION: BORDER CROSSINGS

1   As Edward Said argues in *Covering Islam*, New York, Pantheon, 1981, p. 8:

> Islam seems to engulf all aspects of the diverse Muslim world, reducing them all to a special malevolent and unthinking essence. Instead of analysis and understanding as a result, there can be for the most part only the crudest form of us-versus-them.

A similar prejudice against the 'Orientalist' other is analysed by Partha Mitter with reference to Western attitudes to Indian art and religion; see her *Much Maligned Monsters: A History of European Reactions to Indian Art*, Chicago and London, University of Chicago Press, 1992.

2   The spectre of slavery represents a very visible instance of the 'return of the repressed'. Black–white scenarios of inclusion/exclusion are regularly displayed in TV dramas like the O. J. Simpson or Rodney King versus LA Police trials. In these cases we find scenarios where, at a symbolic-imaginary level, the hyphenated pact struck between Afro- and American almost comes unstuck – the final verdict hanging delicately on a court ruling (the rule of law, once again, as ultimate arbiter of American society). The repeated screenings of the race drama on TV, in the cinema and in courtroom broadcasts are too numerous to mention here; though Spielberg's recent reflective feature film *Amistad* is a good example of how the Constitution is still recalled by way of rehearsing the integrative pact between descendants of African slaves and American Pilgrims. In this context, it is ironic to recall how the Constitution, drafted almost one and half centuries after the Mayflower Compact, also served to separate voting citizens from nonvoting ones – Indians and slaves need not apply. Some of the framers of this Constitution even practised slavery and fought in the Indian wars. In short, the aliens over against whom the 'Americans' were

defining their national identity had now expanded beyond the English and the Indians (later to be renamed, ironically, 'Native Americans') to include the growing population of imported black slaves and propertyless immigrants. Some of these issues are dealt with by Robert Burgoyne in *Film Nation: Hollywood Looks at U.S. History*, Minneapolis, Minnesota University Press, 1977.

3 Borders are crucial to the entire US story. For if the border with Canada marks the expulsion of competing 'others' (Indians, French and Colonial British) northwards after the French and Indian Wars and the War for Independence, the border with Mexico marks the expulsion of similar competitors southwards after the Mexican Wars and especially the famous story of sacrificial martyrdom at the Alamo (where the legendary American pathfinder Davy Crockett, 'king of the wild frontier', entered the pantheon of American heroes). Popular campaigns against illegal aliens, as noted above, are obsessed with the notion of 'porous borders'. And on a more academic front, investigators of alien abduction testimonies like Professor John Mack of Harvard and colleagues often speak of 'borderline' experiences upsetting our assumptions about the frontiers separating 'real' from 'unreal'. See *PEER Perspectives: Expanding Awareness of Extraordinary Experiences*, no. 3, 2000, p. 12; see also John Mack and Budd Hopkins, *A Dialogue on the Alien Encounter Experience*, PEER Perspectives, Cambridge, MA, 1999, and John Mack, *Passport to the Cosmos: Human Transformation and Alien Encounters*, PEER, Cambridge, MA, 1999. Aliens are called, amongst other things, 'daemon realities' by the authors of PEER Perspectives, no. 3, p. 12.

4 Michel Foucault, 'The Order of Discourse', in R. Young (ed.), *Unifying the Text: A Poststructuralist Reader*, London, Routledge, 1981, p. 60. See also Andrew Gibson's excellent commentary on this theme in 'Narrative and Monstrosity' in *Toward a Postmodern Theory of Narrative*, Edinburgh, Edinburgh University Press, 1999, pp. 238–9, and Timothy Beal's more theological discussion of this theme in *Religion and its Monsters* (London and New York, Routledge, 2001), where he uses some central definitions of the monstrous by Mircea Eliade and Rudolph Otto to explore the dual phenomena of religion as horror and horror as religion. His basic understanding of the monstrous, based on Freud's notion of the 'uncanny', is that of 'otherness within

sameness'. I am greatly indebted to Foucault, Kristeva and Gibson for much of this analysis.

5 M. Foucault, *The History of Sexuality*, vol. 1, London, Penguin, 1990, pp. 78, 90–1.

6 Gibson, 'Narrative and Monstrosity', p. 239. At best, innovative and exploratory narratives can help us learn to live with our aliens and monsters so that we may scapegoat others less and come to accept ourselves as strangers-to-ourselves. And this pertains as much to those monsters we project into outer space (extra-terrestrials) as to those we expel under ground (for example infra-terrestrials like the dinosaurs of *Jurassic Park*, the shark of *Jaws* or more human monsters like Dracula, Frankenstein's monster or the various anti-heroes of the criminal underground). The infra-terrestrials go back in turn to such ancient biblical monsters as the Leviathan and Behemoth in Job or the dragon in John.

7 See in particular the Raelian web-site (www.rael.org) and related videos and publications, which argue that 'extraterrestrials . . . are Elohim, the God of the Bible. They are eternal. They come from another planet. They created humanity scientifically. They have sent their last prophet Rael. They are coming!'. The political catch-cry of this group is, interestingly, 'Peace on earth through a worldwide government. Love of the differences'. See *The Face of God*, USAR, Miami, 1973. Other New Age gurus, besides Rael, have construed God as an alien: David Koresh, for example, referred to the New Jerusalem as an extra-terrestrial spacecraft, while the equally paranoid guru Paul Brunton declared that he and Jesus were astral bodies descended from a realm inhabited by superior beings. One might also cite in this context the cult phenomenon of Superman as a preternatural 'stranger' who drops from the sky to a pasture in Smallville, Kansas, to fight for 'Truth, Justice and the American Way'. The sentiment of religious aura generated by the arrival of alien beings in films such as *ET* or *Close Encounters of the Third Kind* is also relevant to this alternative tendency to angelise – as opposed to demonise – aliens. This conforms to a certain logic, observed by René Girard in *Violence and the Sacred*, of sacrificial transformation whereby the 'outsider' may be treated alternately as reviled scapegoat or revered divinity.

8 I shall be attempting to outline such a hermeneutics of critical

discernment in my more academically specialised sequel to this book entitled *Strangers, Gods and Monsters* (London and New York, Routledge, forthcoming 2002).

ELEVEN NARRATIVE MATTERS

1   London and New York, Granta, 2000.

2   See Fredric Jameson, *Postmodernism, or the Cultural Logic of Late Capitalism*, London, Verso, 1991 and Paul Virilio, *Open Sky*, London, Verso, 1997.

3   A. Robbe-Grillet, *Snapshots and Towards a New Novel*, cited by Christopher Nash, 'Literature's Onslaught on Narrative', in *Narrative in Culture: The Uses of Storytelling in the Sciences, Philosophy and Literature*, ed. Christopher Nash, London, Routledge, 1990, p. 203.

4   C. Vogler, *The Writer's Journey: Mythic Structure for Writers*, 2nd edn, Studio City, CA, Michael Wiese Publications, 1998. Bruno Bettelheim makes a similar point in his psychoanalytic account of storytelling, *The Uses of Enchantment*, London, Penguin, 1978; as does Joseph Campbell from the perspective of comparative mythology and depth psychology, in *The Hero with a Thousand Faces*, New York, Balantine Books, 1966.

5   See Paul Ricoeur, 'On Interpretation', in *The Continental Philosophy Reader*, ed. R. Kearney and M. Rainwater, London, Routledge, 1996, p. 139f. See also 'Can Fictional Narratives be True?', where Ricoeur expands on Kant's analysis of the productive imagination. Ricoeur's major critique of Kant, which I endorse, is that by confining the narrative functions of synthesis and schematism to the inner sense of imagination, he ignores the essentially 'intersubjective' aspect of narrative. See my analysis of Heidegger's controversial reading of Kantian imagination in *The Wake of Imagination*, London and New York, Routledge, 1988. See also here E. Husserl's *On the Phenomenology of the Consciousness of Internal Time* (Dordrecht, Kluwer, 1990), M. Heidegger's *Kant and the Problem of Metaphysics* (Bloomington, IN, Indiana University Press, 1962), H.-G. Gadamer's *Truth and Method* (New York, Continuum, 1975) and David Carr's *Time, Narrative and History* (Bloomington, IN, Indiana University Press, 1986).

6   A. MacIntyre, *After Virtue*, Notre Dame, IN, Notre Dame University Press, 1981, p. 117. I am indebted here to the illuminating commentary by Guignon, 'Narrative Explanation in Psychotherapy', p. 569. A similar point is made by Charles Taylor when he argues that a basic

condition for 'making sense of ourselves is to grasp our life in terms of a *narrative*', for in order to have a sense of who we are now 'we have to have a notion of how we have become and of where we are going' (*Sources of the Self: The Making of Modern Identity*, Cambridge, MA, Harvard University Press, 1989, p. 47). Taylor agrees with thinkers like Ricoeur and MacIntyre that the notion of moral identity is intimately linked with that of narrative identity. In our search for some meaning for our life considered as a whole we want the future to make the past 'a part of a life-story which has sense or purpose, to take it up into a meaningful unity'(p. 51). But it is just this search for narrative unity and identity that Lawrence Langer so vehemently opposes in *Holocaust Testimonies*, where he speaks of the Shoah as a wound from an absent and inaccessible past which no amount of narrative remembering can ever heal or redeem in the present: 'The raw material of oral Holocaust narratives, in content and manner of presentation, resists the organizing impulse of moral theory and art'(p. 204).

7 See Guignon, 'Narrative Explanation in Psychotherapy', p. 559f. and P. Ricoeur, 'Life in Quest of Narrative', in *On Paul Ricoeur: Narrative and Interpretation*, ed. D. Wood, London, Routledge, 1991.

8 See Ricoeur: 'Between living and recounting, a gap – however small it may be – is opened up. Life is lived, history is recounted'(*The Continental Philosophy Reader*, ed. Kearney and Rainwater, p. 141). See also Ricoeur, 'Life in Quest of Narrative', p. 31:

> If it is true that fiction is only completed in life and that life can be understood only through the stories that we tell about it, then an examined life, in the sense of the word as we have borrowed it from Socrates, is a life recounted.

9 The recounted life entails both poetics and ethics, both freedom of imagination and responsibility to the real. But this complementarity of narrative poetics and ethics is not a matter of identity; it is by guarding over each other's distinctness that poetics and ethics best serve each other's mutual interests. While a poetics of narrative reminds us that the real is reconstructed, an ethics of narrative reminds us that it is given. But a poetics of mimesis can also serve an ethics of the real by recalling the reference of all narrative to (1) the life-world of the author it originally prefigures, before it configures it as an emplotted

text, and (2) the life-world of the reader which it refigures as it returns from the text to the world of action. This proves the extremism of Roland Barthes's maxim that 'le fait n'a jamais qu'une existence linguistique'.

10   See the pioneering work of Gloriana Davenport and other collaborators on research into future narrative forms and timelines for general audiences at the Media Lab, MIT, Cambridge, Massachusetts. In particular, G. Davenport, 'Your own Virtual Storyworld', *Scientific American*, November 2000, pp. 79–82; G. Davenport, B. Barry et al., 'Synergistic Storyscapes and Constructionist Cinematic Sharing', IBM *Systems Journal*, vol. 39, nos 3–4, 2000, pp. 456–69; G. Davenport and M. Murtaugh, 'Automatist Storyteller Systems and the Shifting Sands of Story', IBM *Systems Journal*, 1997.

11   P. Ricoeur, 'Can Fictional Narratives be True?', in *Analecta Husserliana*, ed. A.-T. Tymienecka, Dordrecht, Reidel, vol. 14, 1983, p. 11. Ricoeur adds this intriguing query: 'And the question, then, is whether in another sense of the word true and truth, history and fiction may be said to be equally "true", although in ways as different as their referential claims are themselves different.' See here the fascinating articles by D. McCloskey, B. Jackson, J. Bernstein, R. Harré and G. Myers in the section entitled 'Narrative and Fact', in *Narrative in Culture: The Uses of Storytelling in the Sciences, Philosophy and Literature*, ed. C. Nash, London and New York, Routledge, 1990. For us to address properly the much-neglected role played by narrative in science would require a separate book in its own right. But I do not underestimate its crucial importance.

12   See the interview with Paul Ricoeur, 'The Creativity of Language' in my *States of Mind: Dialogues with Contemporary Thinkers*, Edinburgh, Edinburgh University Press, and New York, New York University Press, 1997, p. 218. See also Ricoeur, 'Can Fictional Narratives be True?', where he offers a very useful summary of the tension between the 'referential' and 'fictional' claims of storytelling, pp. 5–6:

> A full recognition of the referential dimension of fictional narratives will be made more plausible if the fictional component of history writing has also been previously acknowledged. . . . It is not foreign to the general trend of 'imaginative reconstruction' in the writing of history. This expression comes from Collingwood, even though he

insisted on the task of 'reenactment' in historical knowledge. Thus, while the whole neo-Kantian school of the philosophy of history, as presented for example by Raymond Aron in *The German Critical Philosophy of History*, tends to enlarge the gulf between what actually happened and what we historically know, it is mainly by means of a kind of transfer from the theory of narratives in literary criticism to history considered as literary artifact that history writing has begun to be reassessed along the categories of what may be called semiotics, symbolics, or poetics. In this regard, the influence of Northrop Frye's *The Anatomy of Criticism* and Kenneth Burke's *A Grammar of Motives* has been overwhelmingly decisive, especially when taken in conjunction with such works as Gombrich's critique of the visual arts in *Art and Illusion* and Erich Auerbach's great *Mimesis: The Representation of Reality in Western Literature*. From these works emerged a general concept of the 'fictive' representation of 'reality' whose scope is broad enough to be applied also to history writing as well as to fiction. Hayden White calls . . . the explanatory procedures which history has in common with other literary expressions of story-telling, Poetics. . . . The historian, according to his point of view, does not merely tell a story. He makes an entire set of events, considered as a completed whole, into a story.

Ricoeur offers the following response to the enigma of storytelling's dual role as (a) *fictional invention* and (b) *representation of reality*:

> As fictive as the historical text may be, its claim is to be a representation of reality. And its way of asserting this claim is to support it by the verificationist procedures proper to history as a science. In other words, history is both a literary artifact and a representation of reality. It is a literary artifact to the extent that, like all literary texts, it tends to assume the status of a self-contained system of symbols. It is a representation of reality to the extent that the world that it depicts – which is the 'work's world' – is assumed to stand for some actual occurrences in the 'real' world.

(p. 7)

13 J. M. Coetzee, *The Lives of Animals*, Princeton, NJ, Princeton University Press, 1999, pp. 34–5. Julian Barnes makes a similar point (*A History of the World in 10 and a Half Chapters*, New York, Vintage):

You can't love someone without imaginative sympathy, without beginning to see the world from another point of view. You can't be a good lover, a good artist or a good politician without this capacity (you can get away with it, but that's not what I mean). Show me the tyrants who have been great lovers.

(p. 241)

14 *The Good Listener*, London, Weidenfeld and Nicolson, 1998, p. 228.

15 This call to recognize and remember through narration is, of course, equally central to the whole biblical tradition, summed up in the Hebrew summons 'Remember!'(*Zakhor!*) It is invoked in countless verses of Scripture including Sirach 44: 9–13:

Let us now sing the praises of famous men, our ancestors in their generations. Some of them have left behind a name, so that others declare their praise. But of others there is no memory; they have perished as though they had never existed; they have become as though they had never been born, they and their children after them.

More specifically, the Christian religion is explicitly based on narrative testimony – see Luke 1:1–4:

Since many have undertaken to compile a narrative of the events that have been fulfilled among us, just as those who were eyewitnesses from the beginning and ministers of the word have handed them down to us, I too have decided, after investigating everything accurately anew, to write it down in an orderly sequence for you, most excellent Theophilus, so that you may realize the certainty of the teachings you have reached.

16 Other formative dictionary definitions of the marvellously ambiguous French term *histoire* include the following: (a) 'C'est une narration continuée de choses vraies, grandes and publiques, écrite avec esprit, avec éloquence et avec jugement pour l'instruction des particuliers and des Princes and pour le bien de la société civile. La vérité et l'exactitude sont l'âme de l'histoire'(*Dictionnaire français*, by P. Richelet, 1680); (b) 'Narration des actions et des choses dignes de mémoire' (*Dictionnaire de L'Académie Française*, 1694); (c) 'Recherche, connaissance, reconstruction du passé de l'humanité sous son aspect général ou sous des aspects particuliers, selon le lieu, l'époque, le point de vue

choisi . . . Evolution de l'humanité à travers son passé, son présent, son avenir . . . Evolution concernant une personne ou une chose' (*Trésor de langue française*), 'Histoire . . . contient depuis la latinité (*historia*) l'idée de "récit" fondé sur l'établissement de faits observés (étymologiquement, "vus") ou inventés'. For a fasinating discussion of these and other definitions and descriptions of the double-sidedness of history, see *Face à l'histoire*, Petit Journal du Centre Beaubourg, Paris, 1997. For an interesting analysis of the role of memory in history see Jacques Le Goff, *History and Memory*, New York, Columbia University Press, 1992.

17 Tolkien, 'On Fairy-Stories', p. 60.

18 Paul Ricoeur argues that a poetics of historical imagination requires a special 'hermeneutics of historicity' to assess the respective referential claims of fictional and historical narratives in the light of a specific ontological 'form of life' covering our use of narrative language; see 'Can Fictional Narrtives be True?', pp. 11–17; also *Time and Narrative*, vol. 3, especially the chapter on 'The Interweaving of Fiction and History'; see also the critical exchanges between Ricoeur, David Carr and Charles Taylor on this subject, 'Discussion: Ricoeur on Narrative', in *On Paul Ricoeur: Narrative and Interpretation*, ed. D. Wood, London, Routledge, 1991, pp. 160–87). David Carr develops these arguments in his very useful and insightful book, *Time, Narrative and History*, especially pp. 110–22, 153f.

19 See C. Guignon's critical review of this extreme position in 'Narrative Explanation in Psychotherapy', pp. 562–661.

20 H. White, *Metahistory*, Baltimore, The Johns Hopkins University Press, p. 39.

21 Ibid., p. 42. See also White's more moderate but still ultimately relativist-constructivist position in 'Historical Emplotment and the Problem of Truth', in S. Friedlander (ed.), *Probing the Limits of Representation: Nazism and the 'Final Solution'*, Cambridge, MA, Harvard University Press, 1992, pp. 37–53. For a more ethically persuasive version of the pragmatist approach to historical truth see Richard Rorty, 'Truth without Correspondence to Reality', *Philosophy and Social Hope*, London, Penguin, 1999.

22 S. Friedlander, introduction to *Probing the Limits of Representation*, pp. 7, 10. I am also indebted here to the discussion of this theme in two other articles in this edited volume, namely, Perry Anderson, 'On

Emplotment', pp. 54–65; and Amos Funkenstein, 'History, Counter-history, and Narrative', pp. 66–81. See in particular Funkenstein's pertinent comments, p. 79:

> what makes one story more 'real' than another? . . . what distinguishes
> a legitimate revision from a revisionist confabulation? . . . No
> historiographical endeavour may presume to 'represent' reality – if by
> representation we mean a corresponding system of things and their
> signs. Every narrative is, in its way, an exercise in 'worldmaking'. But it
> is not arbitrary. If the narrative is true, reality, whatever its definition,
> must shine through. . . . Closeness to reality can be neither measured
> nor proven by a waterproof algorithm. It must be decided from case to
> case without universal criteria. Everything in a narrative – factual
> content, form, images, language – may serve as indicators.

23 Barnes, *A History of the World in 10 and a Half Chapters*, p. 240.
24 Deborah Lipstadt, 'Canaries in the Mine: Holocaust Denial and the Limited Power of Reason', *Denying the Holocaust: The Growing Assault on Truth and Memory*, New York, Free Press, 1993.
25 Cited in Friedlander, *Probing the Limits of Representation*, p. 20.
26 See P. Ricoeur, 'Life in Quest of Narrative', pp. 22–3. See also my own related studies, 'The Narrative Imagination', *Poetics of Modernity: Toward a Hermeneutic Imagination*, Atlantic Heights, NJ, Humanities Press, 1997, and 'Narrative Imagination – The Ethical Challenge', *Poetics of Imagining – Modern to Postmodern*, new edn, Edinburgh, Edinburgh University Press and New York, Fordham Press, 1998, pp. 241–57.
27 Primo Levi, *Survival in Auschwitz*, New York, Simon and Schuster, 1993, p. 9.
28 See Michael Bell, 'How Primordial is Narrative?', in Nash, *Narrative in Culture*, p. 197:

> Narrative can embody, and thus objectify or vindicate, a form of life but
> it cannot of itself either create, or compel acceptance of, that form of
> life. In its fundamental terms it has to appeal to the reader's consent as
> an existential given. In sum, then, narrative meaning exists dialectically
> in the tension between its world and the world of the reader.

See also Ricoeur, 'Can Fictional Narrative be True?', p. 13:

> Storytelling displays its imaginative skill at the level of a human

experience which is already 'communalized'. Plots, characters, thematic elements, etc. are forms of a life which is really a common life. In this respect, autobiographies, memoirs, and confessions are only subsections of a narrative arc which as a whole describes and redescribes human action in terms of interactions.

29 See Christopher Nash, 'Slaughtering the Subject: Literature's Assault on the Subject', in *Narrative in Culture*, p. 216:

> With any consistent obliteration . . . of discrete persons as agents of discrete events and intentions – or with any description of the subject as simply a manifestation of impersonal collective forces, we can't hope either to account intelligibly for change, explain to ourselves how we feel ourselves to be in disagreement with someone else, or hold anyone responsible for his or her acts.

And as a result, 'social interaction and political action become incomprehensible'. See also my essay, 'Ethics and the Narrative self', in *The Modern Subject*, ed. D. M. Christensen and S. Meyer, Centre for the Study of European Civilisation at the University of Bergen, 1996, pp. 48–62.

30 See Paul Ricoeur, *Time and Narrative*, vol. 3, Chicago, University of Chicago Press, 1988; *Oneself as Another*, Chicago, Chicago University Press, 1992. For a lucid commentary on this *ipse/idem* distinction see Bernard Dauenhauer, *Paul Ricoeur: The Promise and Risk of Politics*, New York and Oxford, Brown and Littlefield, 1998, pp. 110f., 120–2.

31 Langer, *Holocaust Testimonies*, p. 183. See also the insightful contributions to this debate in *Evil After Postmodernism: Histories, Narratives, Ethics*, ed. Jennifer Geddes, London and New York, Routledge, 2001: in particular the essays by Berel Lang, 'Evil Inside and Outside History: The Post-Holocaust vs. the Postmodern' and Roger Shattuck, 'Narrating Evil', and my own 'Others and Aliens: Between Good and Evil'.

32 Langer, *Holocaust Testimonies*, p. 182. It is, however, because Langer so vigorously underscores all the obstacles to normal ethical narrative and judgement in the Holocaust testimonies – repudiating the cathartic, compensatory or redemptive functions of storytelling – that his work serves as such an indispensable limit-case for my own attempts to defend and promote narrative.

33 Ricoeur, 'Can Fictional Narratives be True?', p. 14. Ricoeur

acknowledges his debt here not only to Heidegger's analysis of historicity in *Being and Time* but to Hans-Georg Gadamer's notion of *Wirkungsgeschichte* or 'effective history' in *Truth and Method*. See, for example, Gadamer's claim that 'a proper hermeneutics would have to demonstrate the effectivity of history within understanding itself' (*Truth and Method*, London, Sheed and Ward, 1973, p. 267).

34 Ricoeur, 'Can Fictional Narratives be True?', pp. 15–16.

35 Richard Rorty, 'Philosophers, Novelists and Intercultural Companions', *Cultural Otherness*, ed. A. Niyogi Balslev, Atlanta, Scholars Press, 1991, p. 118. I am grateful to Mark Dooley for bringing these citations to my attention.

36 Rorty, 'On Ethnocentrism', *Objectivity, Relativism and Truth* (Cambridge, Cambridge University Press, 1991).

37 Ricoeur, *Time and Narrative*, vol. 1, p. 59. As Ricoeur notes, the strategy of persuasion undertaken by the narrator

> is aimed at giving the reader a vision of the world that is never ethically neutral, but that rather implicitly or explicitly induces a new evaluation of the world and of the reader as well. In this sense, narrative already belongs to the ethical field in virtue of its claim – inseparable from its narration – to ethical justice. Still, it belongs to the reader, now an agent, an initiator of action, to choose among the multiple proposals of ethical justice brought forth by the reading.
>
> (*Time and Narrative*, vol. 3, 1986, p. 249)

Even when stories set out to overturn the inherited ethical system of establishment value, they do so, almost invariably, from an opposing or alternative set of evaluations. 'Poetics does not stop borrowing from ethics, even when it advocates the suspension of all ethical judgment or its ironic inversion. The very project of ethical neutrality presupposes the original ethical quality of action'(*Time and Narrative*, vol. 1, p. 59).

Index

191 **On** Stories